Weldon Kees

Twayne's United States Authors Series

Warren French, Editor

Indiana University

TUSAS 484

WELDON KEES (1947)
Photograph courtesy of
The Editor of POETRY

Weldon Kees

By William T. Ross

University of South Florida

Twayne Publishers • *Boston*

Weldon Kees

William T. Ross

Copyright © 1985 by G. K. Hall & Company

All Rights Reserved
Published by Twayne Publishers
A Division of G. K. Hall & Co.
A publishing subsidiary of ITT
70 Lincoln Street
Boston, Massachusetts 02111

Book Production by Lyda E. Kuth
Book Design by Barbara Anderson

Printed on permanent/durable acid-free
paper and bound in the United States of
America.

Library of Congress Cataloging in Publication Data

Ross, William T.
    Weldon Kees.

(Twayne's United States author series; TUSAS 484)
Bibliography: p. 144
Includes index.
    1. Kees, Weldon, 1914–1955?—Criticism and interpreta-
tion.   I. Title.   II. Series.
PS3521.E285Z87   1985   811'.52   84–15734
ISBN 0–8057–7437–8 (alk. paper)

Contents

About the Author

William T. Ross is an associate professor of English at the University of South Florida in Tampa. He received his Ph.D. from the University of Virginia. His special interests include romantic and modern literature and stylistics. He has published articles on Iris Murdoch and George Orwell as well as several theoretical explorations of the nature of exposition. Before coming to South Florida, he served on the faculties of the University of Virginia and Mary Washington College. Since September of 1979, he has been his department's director of graduate studies.

Preface

Had Weldon Kees never written poetry, the art form for which he is most remembered, his would still be a fascinating life. Few men have managed to cram so many careers and interests in a mere twenty years of adult life. Writer of short fiction and film scripts, abstract-expressionist painter and collagist, photographer, cinematographer, musician, composer, critic of art and popular music—Kees's interests seemed to embrace almost all the arts. And far from being an ineffectual dilettante, he managed to make significant contributions in almost every area he touched. Renaissance men are rare in the twentieth century, and Kees would make a fascinating study in the psychology of creativity, for surely few have managed to master the vision and idiom of so many diverse forms in such a short length of time.

The special fascination of Kees as a poet is not hard to define. Born in 1913, he came of age when the major revolutions in modern poetry were firmly established. He did nothing to bring about another revolution, but he shows more clearly than any other American poet of his generation how the forms and techniques available to him can be utilized and manipulated to create a voice at once distinctive and firmly within the new tradition. (He also shows, over the course of his poetic career, how a poet can grow within that tradition.) From T. S. Eliot, for example, he learned how to use the "mythic method"—Eliot's term for the juxtaposition of images from past and present to make an ironic comment on modern life. From Auden, he learned how to comment on the most distressing cultural situations in an urbane, even sardonic tone. Of course, he learned much more from both, and from a less well defined inheritance he was able to derive the techniques that made him capable of writing poetry that appears to have the syntax and lucidity of prose and still retains a definite poetic resonance. He employed the European traditions of expressionistic and surrealistic imagery absolutely essential for the depiction of the absurdity and horror he found in the modern world. Finally, he discovered how (sometimes) to make a poem evolve its total meaning through the play of its images and symbols, how to make it surrender its meaning slowly and only after the total involvement of the reader.

If Kees managed, however, to find a unique voice to embody this inheritance, his was also a voice of despair. And this despair, too, was also partially inherited. Eliot's *Waste Land,* after all, was the most discussed serious poem of the period; and its images of a culture perishing in its own despair, disbelief, and meaninglessness represented the horror many intellectuals felt in examining their own times. An examination of Kees's work leaves no doubt that he shared this horror fully, so fully that it is a wonder that he was able to exercise the aesthetic distance necessary to keep that horror confined to formal poetic structures rather than letting it spill over into diatribes and incoherent shrieks.

Such artistic control and discipline is even more of a wonder when one realizes that Eliot (and Auden and many other poets of the culture crisis) could see, however dimly at times, a way out of the dilemma. For the early Eliot there was at least the assurance that the past had been better, more assured, more meaningful; for the later Eliot there was the belief that modern angst could be cured by a renewal of traditional Christian faith. For others, of course, the answer lay in the twentieth-century substitutes for faith: ideology or psychoanalysis. Kees stands almost alone among those who came to maturity between the two wars in never having given any assent to either revivified religion or Marx or Freud. The answer to the modern malaise— though Kees is not always sure that it is distinctively modern— did not lie either in a return to the past or in any of the currently fashionable solutions.

And though he was a man of culture, capable of participating in what is called the life of the mind, the kind of man of letters who can turn out book reviews on the latest "thoughtful" analysis of our cultural or intellectual situation, he could find no consolation in such culture. Since at least Matthew Arnold's time, some had been able to hold that "the best that had been thought and said"—that is, the intellectual inheritance of the Western world—was sufficient substitute for a lost supernatural faith, sufficient reassurance that man could indeed find the wisdom necessary to save himself and be his consolation. Such so-called humanism held no appeal for Kees. There is another solution, one especially open to the artist— that of aestheticism. One can proclaim, as Yeats and Wallace Stevens did in different and highly complex ways, that "Beauty is truth, truth beauty" and find consolation in the richness and pattern of art. Given Kees's lifelong devotion to a number of the arts, one would certainly think Kees an ideal candidate for this point of view. In fact, it is never even considered in his poetry. The horrors of the world were real, the horrors of the individual psyche were real, and the consolatory power of art could not erase them.

Partly what art could not erase or exorcise was the past. The most fascinating single element in Kees is the way in which he keeps returning to the past. He knows that what we are today results from the past and yet we cannot make any sense of the past. This does not mean, of course, that the past does not haunt us, cripple us. But there is simply no way to turn it into something useful or to consign it to oblivion.

Kees defines the past in the widest possible terms. All elements of it impinge upon us. The historical past helps constitute and explain the catalog of horrors that is the objective present. And our personal past—a record for Kees of disappointments and failed relationships—reinforces the malaise brought on by our awareness of the outside world and reassures us that we will never find consolation or redemption. Even the infantile or Freudian past is recognized by Kees as a source of much of our unhappiness, although he tends to emphasize the contribution made by the more objective horrors of the real world— horrors psychoanalysis can hardly erase.

And yet he continues to return to the past as his subject, insisting on its reality but also underscoring the impossibility of dealing with it. There is something absolutely heroic about his continuing to examine a disease for which he is convinced there is no cure.

Perhaps the lack of a solution, the lack of any real salvational possibility in the modern world, led to Kees's presumed suicide on 19 July 1955. Or perhaps the suicide had more to do with personal difficulties than with cosmic dilemmas. We will probably never know for sure. What is certain is that almost until his last days, despite his profoundly pessimistic view of the world, he was practicing the craft of poetry and improving his talent. This study will devote most of its space to an examination of that talent.

What is perhaps surprising is that Kees actually began his career as a writer by publishing short fiction. Over a period of about six years, he published at least thirty short stories in various little magazines and reviews of the 1930s and 1940s. With one exception, the poetry and fiction have little in common. Kees seems to have come into the inheritance of the kind of modernism described above simultaneously with his decision to make poetry his dominant form of literary expression. The short stories do not reflect any sort of cosmic uneasiness or brooding over history, but are rather constructed in the manner of the modish regional satire of Sinclair Lewis and the even more modish economic determinism of the Depression era. Admittedly not on a par with the poetry, they do not deserve to be entirely neglected; for they reveal, if nothing else, how the same mind can, given the choice of literary traditions, produce work of vastly different caliber.

The present volume is designed to serve as an introduction to the literary endeavors of Weldon Kees. In the brief first chapter I offer a sketch of his life and provide some samples of his nonfictional prose—art and book reviews, general essays on culture, etc. These selections help confirm the basic continuity of his interests and outlook. The second chapter is devoted entirely to Kees's published short fiction. I have tried to arrange the consideration topically in order to show some of the various attitudes toward his material Kees employed. But the fiction is admittedly not superior material on the whole, and I have not felt obliged to include a discussion of every story.

The next three chapters concern themselves, in succession, with the heart of Kees's achievement, his three published volumes of poetry. Given the relative brevity of Kees's career, a topical rather than a chronological scheme of development might have been indicated; however, I think there is genuine progression in Kees and, often, genuine improvement in depth of ability from volume to volume. If this is true, then any topical arrangement would be forced, in evaluation, to become chronological.

Within each of the three chapters I try to enumerate the major thematic concerns, analyze and evaluate all the truly significant poems in the volume, and point out some of the interesting failures as well. I try to apportion more space to those poems whose length or complexity or accomplishment deserves it.

The final chapter of the book is concerned with a selection of poems not included in any of the three volumes published during his lifetime and with his still unpublished play, "The Waiting Room." "The Waiting Room" remains unpublished and unproduced, even though several sources have announced it to the world. It is also Kees's only mature attempt, so far as we know, at drama. For these reasons I have decided to include it in my discussion. For equally good reasons, I believe, I have elected to exclude any other previously unpublished material or to obligate myself to deal with every one of the published poems. Kees is a relatively unknown figure, despite his obvious success. It is far better to provide an introduction to those items of his which are relatively accessible and either outright successes or interesting failures than to attempt to be encyclopedic. The sort of homage represented by such all-encompassing endeavors, one hopes, awaits Kees in the future.

I am indebted to the authors of the handful of serious commentaries on Kees which have appeared over the past twenty years. I have cited some in my text, included all in my bibliography. While I hope my account of Kees's accomplishments is fuller and more comprehensive, I have not tried to spark any spurious disagreements between myself and other commentators. Kees deserves more critics, but he is undoubtedly blessed in the ones he has had so far.

Selections from *The Collected Poems of Weldon Kees* are reprinted by permission of the University of Nebraska Press © 1962, 1975 by the University of Nebraska Press. Since all citations are from this single source, I have not footnoted every poem as it comes up for discussion. In citing "The Waiting Room," I have silently emended obvious errors in the manuscript copy.

I am indebted to the following people for help in my research: Charles Baxter, Maurice Berezov, Thomas B. Brumbaugh, Fritz Bultman, John R. Clark, Stephen Cox, Irving Deer, Dana Gioia, Gary Goldberg, Clayton Hoagland, Mrs. Lee Hemingway, Donald Justice, H. Christian Kiefer, Robert E. Knoll, James Laughlin, Jack B. Moore, Kent Paul, Harry Roskolenko, Jurgen Ruesch, M.D., Marguerite C. Rawdon Smith, Rudolph Umland, Joseph B. Wheelwright, M.D., Robert Wilbur, and William Zander.

Finally, I am especially grateful to Anniece, David, and Poco.

William T. Ross

University of South Florida

Chronology

Chapter One

The Life and Careers of Weldon Kees

Some Biographical Facts

Weldon Kees was born on 24 February 1914 in Beatrice, Nebraska, the only child of John A. and Sarah Green Kees.[1] His parents appear to have been sturdy midwestern stock, with his father a second-generation German-American and his mother able to trace her lineage back to the Mayflower. The parents were sensitive, cultured individuals, and Weldon must have grown up with the typical middle-class respect for religion (Presbyterian, in this case), hard work, and polite, genteel culture. He was a rather frail but precocious child and apparently did all right in school. Later he would attend Doane College, where he felt stifled, and then spend a year at the University of Missouri before getting his degree at the University of Nebraska in 1935. Twenty years later, on 18 July 1955, Weldon Kees presumably committed suicide by jumping off the Golden Gate bridge. Remarks to his friends left open the possibility that, instead of ending the present life, he might go to Mexico in search of a new one. But the finding of his abandoned car on an approach to the bridge convinced most that he had chosen the former alternative.

In the twenty years of his adult life, Weldon Kees managed to pursue a variety of successful careers. The career that concerns us primarily, and for which he is principally remembered, is that of a poet. Kees's poetry has never been as well known as it deserves, but it has always found its admirers, especially among fellow-poets such as Kenneth Rexroth, Donald Justice, Howard Nemerov, Stephen Berg, and Robert Mezey. And Donald Justice's pioneering *Collected Poems,* first published in 1960 by a small private press in Iowa, has now seen two editions as a University of Nebraska paperback.[2] But there is much more to Kees's accomplishments. His life, in its multiplicity of interests, is enough to tantalize any serious biographer and to frustrate the author of a critical analysis who can only devote a few pages to charting it. The most amazing single feature of Kees's life was how he was able to move from one discipline to another so effortlessly, becoming accomplished in the new field, it would seem, almost overnight. Even in his first real job, at the Denver Public Library—a job he doubtless took only to earn a living—he managed to become acting director of an important project five years out of college. During the same period, he would switch from the writing of fiction to the writing of poetry and start to be recognized as a fine and serious poet almost immediately. He would have no trouble finding work as a journalist; he would become a painter, a musician, a composer, a photographer, and a filmmaker and manage to do creditable and recognized work in all these areas. His painting even led to his name being linked and his works shown with some of the leading exponents of the (then) new New York school of abstract expressionism. Success does not always breed happiness, and Kees was not a very happy man, but an outline of his career should convince anyone that here was an extraordinarily versatile and gifted individual.

After showing an interest in writing college dramas, Kees began his career as a short-story writer. Between 1934 and 1945 he published at least forty stories. Of these, eight were published in *Prairie Schooner,* a literary journal with a national reputation edited by Lowry Charles Wemberly, one of Kees's instructors at the University of Nebraska. Two stories, "I Should Worry" and "The Evening of the Fourth of July," were published by *New Directions in Prose and Poetry,* one of the most prestigious avant-garde journals of its time, and the latter story is by far Kees's best. Kees also managed to write two novels for which he never found publishers, although the New York publishing firm of Alfred Knopf had an option on one of them. Later, after the war, Kees wrote a one-act play, "The Waiting Room," which has never been published or produced but which has at least gained an admiring comment from Kenneth Rexroth, one of Kees's many literary friends.

During the period when Kees was publishing his short fiction, other things were happening to him as well. He worked on the Federal Writer's Project—a Depression-era WPA undertaking—a position he got in part through the sponsorship of Professor Wemberly. Then he moved to Denver where he began working at the Denver Public Library and acquired a bachelor's degree in library science from the University of Denver. He lived in Denver with his wife, the former Ann Swan, whom he married on 3 October 1937, and to whom he would stay married almost until his disappearance. From 1940–43 Kees was acting director of the Bibliographical Center of Research, Rocky Mountain Region, an agency devoted to fostering cooperation among the libraries of the region and to producing a union or joint catalog of their various collections. But most importantly during these years Kees began writing poetry. And it is obvious from the publication data that Kees's interest in fiction writing was soon replaced by a dedication to poetry. His first poem ("Subtitle") was published in an obscure little magazine, *Signatures,* in 1937. Six years later, his first volume appeared, published by the Colt Press in San Francisco. What is more amazing than the publication of the volume itself is the number of outlets—many prestigious—that Kees was able to find for his poems almost immediately. The *Kenyon Review, Partisan Review,* and *New Directions,* for example, all originally published poems to be found in this first collection.

By 1943, Kees had had as much of the Denver Public Library as he could stand. He moved to New York, finished putting together an anthology of modern satirical verse for which he never found a publisher, and began working for *Time* magazine. Presumably for some physical reason, he was declared unfit for the draft, a classification which did not distress him in the least. The job at *Time,* which consisted of writing for the book review section, did not last out the year, unfortunately, although again the reasons for Kees's losing it are not clear. But his low opinion of most of what he had to review must have softened any regrets he might have had. He quickly found another journalistic job— this time writing scripts for Paramount Newsreels, a position he kept until 1948. Meanwhile, ensconced at various addresses in Greenwich Village and Brooklyn, Kees continued his career as a poet. Proof that he was highly regarded in the field came not only from the increasingly respectable list of journals that were publishing his poems but, in 1947, from the firm of Reynall and Hitchcock, which published his second volume of poems, *The Fall of Magicians.* The firm was a new trade publishing house, fiercely devoted to quality. Among the other books they published in their too short corporate life was Robert Penn Warren's edition of "The Rime of the Ancient Mariner" with an accompanying explication which became one of the most important examples of the New Criticism. They also published the early poetry of Karl Shapiro and Richard Wilbur. Kees was in good company indeed. In 1948 he won the Oscar Blumenthal Award, one of several annual honors conferred by *Poetry* magazine for work published within its pages during the preceding year.

He was also becoming something of a general man of letters. He was always available to write reviews for several New York newspapers, including the *Times;* his advice on authors and selections for anthologies was sought by, for instance, James Laughlin of New Directions. And his career developed yet another dimension in 1949 when he put in a six-month stint as art critic of the *Nation,* replacing Clement Greenberg.

But Kees still had time for other interests. Most interestingly perhaps, he became an abstract-expressionist painter. And just as his career as a poet took off in a hurry, so did his career as a painter. He had several one-man shows, and several in conjunction with some of the better-known painters of the day.

In 1949 Kees had a one-man show at the Peridot gallery in New York which Stuart Preston reviewed favorably in the 6 November *Times.* Preston divided his attention between Kees and Seattle's Mark Tobey, who also had a one-man show at the time. Part of the review is given over to yet another attempt to define abstract expressionism, but Preston has some kind words for Kees: "The abstract shapes are given such aggressive solidity in themselves that the monochromatic backgrounds are forced into becoming the empty space in which the shapes move and have their being." The shapes "are remotely related to human figures, yet there is something sensuous and provocative about their interactions." Finally Kees is praised for his "genuine feeling for paint" and the ability with which he "harmonizes his strong colors."

In November 1979, the Sheldon Art Gallery of the University

of Nebraska, in Lincoln, presented an exhibition of painting, collages, and photographs by Kees. Kees also became something of a jazz pianist during this period and developed a general interest in the history of popular music. In 1951 Kees decided to leave New York and move to San Francisco. His letters of the time make clear that he was trying to get away from the stifling world of literary in-fighting that he felt New York had become. He was no stranger to San Francisco. He had vacationed there, and his first book of poetry had been published there. Again, once settled, his career flourished in many new areas. Perhaps the most tangible result of this move is a volume called *Non-Verbal Communication: Notes on the Visual Perception of Human Nature* by Jurgen Ruesch and Kees. This pioneering study of the language of visual signs was written by Ruesch and edited by Kees. (It was first published in 1956, after Kees's disappearance, and was reissued in 1965. Both editions actually list Kees as coauthor.) Kees also contributed perhaps 150 photographs to the text, many of them capturing brilliant examples of the way signs, furniture arrangements, window displays, etc., manage to communicate social and economic status, geographic location, even world view.

Ruesch, a psychiatrist interested in communication theory, was associated at the time with the University of California at Berkeley. For the university's Langley Porter Institute, Kees made films (he was apparently now adept not only at writing scripts but at operating a camera and directing) illustrating various psychiatric concepts. The most famous, perhaps, *Three Families,* was made in cooperation with the anthropologist Gregory Bateson. It was meant to illustrate Bateson's famous "double-bind" theory of schizophrenia. But Kees's interest in films did not stop there. He also became involved with the beginnings of experimental filmmaking in California. He scored James Broughton's *Adventures of Jimmy,* a film often mentioned in the histories of avant-garde film, but never with any credit to Kees. Kees also made his own experimental film in 1952, *Hotel Apex.* Robert E. Knoll describes it thus:

A camera study of an abandoned hotel building, it is described by its distributor (in Kees' words, no doubt) as "perhaps the first motion picture which has not a trace of any attempt to lend literary meanings to its material." Running only nine minutes, it is a clear example of American expressionist cinematography. It is no less personal than the poems, and if it has no "literary meanings"—paraphrasable content, I suppose—it has considerable psychological meaning. In the film we are shown the details of a decaying building: the filthy sink, the broken windows, the peeling walls, the stairway (there are always stairways in Kees' poems, as there are always peeling walls), the half open doors into cluttered rooms, the littered floor, pipes which no longer carry water, broken roofs which no longer give shelter, locks which neither protect nor isolate. *Hotel Apex* begins and ends with shots of the blank sky.[3]

Kees also lectured on the history of jazz and produced local "high-brow" radio shows. And, of course, he continued to write poetry. His third and last volume, *Poems 1947–1954*, was published in San Francisco in the year of his disappearance.

Obviously Kees was busy in San Francisco. But, unfortunately, he was just as obviously not happy, at least not in the final months. His marriage to Ann was disintegrating and culminated in divorce. Perhaps his poetry is the best comment on his generally pessimistic view of reality, as will become evident in our analysis of it. What is certain, however, is that Kees was especially depressed in the final weeks of his life, that his behavior was often irrational, and that he showed signs of delusions. No one, apparently, doubted him to be capable of the threatened suicide. With a terribly apt symbolism, the 18 July 1955 *New Republic*—dated the day of his disappearance—published his review of Dr. Arnold A. Hutschnecker's *Love and Hate in Human Nature,* in which Kees notes how in our "present atmosphere of distrust, violence, and irrationality . . . so many human beings [murder] themselves—literally or symbolically. . . ."[4]

Criticism, Reviews, and Journalism

Kees's appointment as art critic for the *Nation* was announced in the 5 November 1948 issue, an announcement mainly concerned with bidding adieu to the better-known Clement Greenberg. Kees was identified as a painter, poet, and critic who had written on art for such publications as the *Magazine of Art* and *Partisan Review.* Over the next seven months he produced eight columns. His departure, after the 3 June 1950 issue, was not officially noted in the pages of the journal.

Kees's critical prose proved to be very much like that of the rest of the *Nation:* literate, incisive, assured, and somewhat ironic. (Kees's entire career, in fact, is marked by the high level of competency he seemed to bring from the start of any number of different tasks: art criticism was no exception.) Obviously an apologist for the New York school of abstract expressionism, he proved knowledgeable about the movement, a partisan of it, and familiar with all the abstract painters whose names are now household words. Mixed in with the reviews are bitter comments about the nature of the art world, characterized by alienation. "One is continually astonished," he is led to write on one occasion, "that art persists at all in the face of so much indifference, failure, and isolation."[5] Such is the traditional lament of the avant-garde.

Kees's last column includes an account of a protest against the then conservative Metropolitan Museum's belated attempt to recognize "modern art" by sponsoring a competitive exhibition entitled "American Art Today"—the competition to be judged, in Kees's opinion, by conservatives as likely to recognize the real avant-garde as "the American Legion building a series of marble shrines honoring the memory" of Randolph Bourne, a well-known pacifist. Or "of Baudelaire being voted the favorite poet of the Cicero, Illinois, junior high school." He then reprints a petition deploring the exhibit, signed by him and seventeen other painters—among them, Jackson Pollock, Hans Hoffman, Adolph Gottlieb, Robert Motherwell, Willem de Kooning, and Mark Rothko. The petition, in which the artists announce their refusal to participate in the competition, is tinged with a messianic faith in art not seen in Kees's poetry:

We draw to the attention of these gentlemen the historical fact that, for roughly a hundred years, only advanced art has made any consequential contribution to civilization.[6]

Such hyperbolic claims were not Kees's usual way of operating, but his commitment to the value of modern art is made even clearer in the one review and the one article he published on modern painters in other journals. The review is of Clement Greenberg's *Joan Miro* for *Partisan Review;* the article, on Robert Motherwell, appeared in the *Magazine of Art.* Both celebrate the absence of subject matter in modern art, the absence of

anything except "the business at hand," that is, the painting
itself. But this typical abstract-expressionist concern with "pure"
subject matter gives way in the Motherwell essay to some comments, if not on subject matter, at least on the manifestations
of cultural concern that can be reflected in Motherwell's paintings. Searching for his uniqueness, Kees begins by quoting the
artist as saying he begins painting with a series of mistakes.
"My pictures have layers of mistakes buried in them—an
x-ray would disclose crimes—layers of consciousness, of willing." From this Kees concludes that the source of Motherwell's
unique strength is "division, that schism of the mind that com-
prises so much of our modernity, a rupture from whose conflicts
we may make art or by which we may be destroyed." He goes
on:

In Motherwell, these conflicts define themselves as a declared, full-
fledged and recognized war. On one side are ranged recklessness,
savagery, chance-taking, the accidental, "quickened subjectivity,"
painting, in the words of Miro, "as we make love; a total embrace,
prudence thrown to the wind, nothing held back"; on the other, refine-
ment, discrimination, calculation, taste . . . [i.e.,] layers of consciousness, of willing.[7]

It is not to the point here to argue whether this is really
about the world and not simply the nature of painting, nor
does such argument have much bearing on Kees's poetic career.
The *Magazine of Art* identified Kees not as a painter but as a
"young satiric poet"; and "satiric" or otherwise, Kees usually
makes perfectly clear that his subject matter is the state of the
world. But it is interesting to speculate how much of this elemen-
tal opposition between the forces of daring and those of taste
pervades Kees's work. Kees's poetry, as we shall see, certainly
provides him opportunity for the horrific to embrace the urbane.

Culture Criticism

As might be expected with a poet who could be thought of
as satirical, Kees had his eye on contemporary culture, and in
a few articles managed to prove himself a capable critic of the
cultural scene. The tradition of "reading" public taste, attitudes,

and behavior as indexes of the moral and intellectual strength of a country goes back at least to Matthew Arnold in the mid-nineteenth century. In the late 1940s, the inevitable sign of moral decline was the anti-Communist witch-hunt mentality which was pervading the country as the cold war became the country's new obsession. One of Kees's first significant efforts had to do with an example of such mentality. In the 1 October 1949 issue of the *Nation,* under the general title "Essays and Asides," Kees published a short piece entitled "Dondero and Dada." Dondero turns out to be a congressman "from the Chicago *Tribune* section of Michigan" who had taken upon himself the mission of ridding America of modern art. (Dada, of course, refers to the movement in the arts which holds that the whole world is alogical and irrational and that art should be equally meaningless and nonsensical.) Mr. Dondero was apparently even more stupid than most of the "American Firsters" of the day, and Kees has no trouble in tearing him to shreds. That Mr. Dondero does not realize that the kind of art he despises happens to be Stalin's least favorite makes Kees's job extremely easy. That Mr. Dondero's preference for a certain kind of realism seems to match Stalin's state-approved "Socialist realism" is simply icing on the cake. The two politicians make good bedfellows, as Kees easily demonstrates.

Kees, however, refuses to believe that Mr. Dondero's monumental ignorance is the cause of his alignment with Kremlin thinking. Instead Mr. Dondero's absurdity represents a "Dadaist maneuver of the highest order." And to add to the solemn fun of the absurdity, the American Communist party—which Kees insists is in on the dadaist prank—has "been busy with manifestoes protesting against the Congressman's line" even though most the artists he attacks are precisely the ones "branded in Russia as 'bourgeois formalists' and 'degenerate lackeys of a dying capitalism.' "

But after Kees has had his fun with the congressman, his more serious purpose appears. Kees closes the essay by trying to tell Mr. Dondero what art really is all about, and the defense shows Kees to be strictly in line with the postwar tendency to see art as a formal, apolitical effort. Art is not a weapon, he insists, and those who want to make weapons do not become artists. The man who looks at art and wants to know the political stance of the artist is not really looking at the painting at all. "As painters we have no concern with politics: as men we are in the midst of them." This dualism between painter and man Kees apparently finds sufficiently real to label "a vast individual schizophrenia." If he wants to insist that art is perfectly well nourished and content cut off from politics, Kees's choice of words is not happy. But he is having no more trouble than most left-formalists of the day in formulating a definition. Finally, back on safer ground, he assures Mr. Dondero that no artist of any nationality has ever "attempted to portray [his] country in plain or simple terms. They have been engaged in tasks more arduous, complex, and enduring."[8]

Six years later, on 17 January 1955, Kees reviewed Russell Lynes's *The Tastemakers* for the *New Republic*. Lynes was responsible for the well-known division of American culture into lowbrow, middlebrow, and highbrow, a distinction that seems to bother Kees because it pigeonholes people, not art. He is also bothered by Lynes's dislike for highbrows—that is, for those artists and that part of the audience apt to like abstract-expressionist painting and the more recondite sorts of modern poetry. Kees cannot define taste either, he is forced to admit, but he is quite sure where one should go to find the makers of taste.

We have to assume, in these matters, that some people know more than others—just as we know that Stravinsky knows more about music than the leader of a Boy Scout band in Kansas—that the taste of a Matisse was superior to that of a Rockwell Kent, that Eric von Stroheim's taste ranges wider than Stanley Kramer's or Joe Pasternak's, and that Ezra Pound's goes beyond any of the Benets.[9]

Kees's snobbishness is a good indication of how far the American left—as represented not by the apolitical Kees but by the two leftwing journals of opinion these reviews appear in—had given up any kind of political commitment in literature or any feeling for art for those not so "highbrow." But it is interesting to note that he includes film directors among his comparisons (von Stroheim, Kramer, and Pasternak). Kees never actually wrote on films, but the allusion itself was not exactly natural in those days. It puts Kees in a very select group of essayists (James Agee, Dwight Macdonald, Manny Farber, Robert Warshow) who took films and other manifestations of popular culture seriously.

Kees's only contribution to the criticism of popular culture, however, is a long essay for *Partisan Review* on the subject of popular music. "Muskrat Ramble: Popular and Unpopular Music" is the only one of Kees's essays to be subsequently reprinted.[10] Like much of the criticism of popular arts at the time, Kees's piece suffers from what might be called a golden-age complex. For many film critics, the golden age of the film was the silent period—everything since, or almost everything, is trash. Kees transfers this attitude to popular music, lamenting that the only thing he can find on the radio these days is "a voice not easily distinguishable from Miss Margaret Truman's singing 'At Dawning,' " a program of light classics "played by a feeble string group," and music by the big dance bands. He had been wanting to hear Jelly Roll Morton, but obviously all quality has disappeared. The article is packed with polarized comparisons designed to show the inferiority of the present: Jelly Roll Morton versus Margaret Truman; creative, improvisatory jazz versus the big dance bands; even the old creative Duke Ellington versus the Ellington engaged in musical embroidery work. Indeed, nearly all the greats of popular music are either dead or mere shadows of their former selves. And, in an aside, he both extends and reverses the technique to include comedians. The great comedians, "Lloyd Hamilton, W. C. Fields, Buster Keaton," have "give[n] way to verbalising gagsters: Bob Hope, Milton Berle, Red Skelton." And when they do improve—as Fields did toward the end of his life and as Chaplin was in the process of doing—the audience turns on them. Such betrayal is offered as proof of the ineluctable laws which Kees sees as governing popular taste. To wit: "Epstean's law (people satisfy their needs and desires with the least possible assertion), Gresham's (bad money drives out good money), and the law of diminishing returns" (230).

Alas, as Kees's subsequent attack on bebop makes clear, in the field of popular music there is "total capitulation" to these laws. Somehow, after 1936, everything had gone wrong. Of course, with our own nostalgias more comfortably aimed at the 1940s and 1950s, we would disagree with most of Kees's judgments. But the point to make, once again, is how easily and competently Kees acquired one of the styles of criticism, and how comfortable he seems within its conventions, its patterns of thought and procedure. What should also be noted, however, is Kees's intellectual honesty. When Chandler Brossard reprinted the essay in *The Scene Before You* (1955), Kees appended a footnote in which, in the midst of chronicling even further decay in taste and standards, he manages, apparently, to see some bright spots. Bebop has given way to "progressive" jazz; there is a revival of interest in New Orleans jazz; and many small labels offering quality music seem to be appearing. At least for Kees, the golden-age complex did not turn into a set of cultural blinders.

Finally, as we have already noted, in the 18 July 1955 *New Republic,* Weldon Kees published a review of Dr. Arnold A. Hutschnecker's *Love and Hate in Human Nature,* an example of the type of psychiatric self-help book that had already become one of the staples of the publishing business. Kees, as might be expected, is suspicious of popularized Freudianism, and in fact of Freudianism itself, which, he observes, is not "of much help in understanding or treating schizophrenics." But Kees's main venom is reserved for Dr. Hutschnecker's promotion of the therapeutic value of "self-knowledge." With such self-knowledge, Kees quotes Dr. Hutschnecker, "we are now able to penetrate the mystery of the unconscious itself." Kees is scornful:

Socrates, Proust, and Coleridge, for instance, had more "self-knowledge" and knew more at first hand of love and hate than the Doctor will ever know; . . . they never believed for a minute that "self-knowledge" could, in the long run save them—or us. . . . The liberal assumption that self-knowledge will lead to "adjustment" and "happiness" is a curious one; it is not very inspiriting to see it presented in terms of "science," as Doctor Hutschnecker does. I have frequently wondered what course psychiatry would have taken if it had developed out of the humanities rather than medicine.[11]

But the speculation, like most of Kees's, is not a hopeful one: he had already intimated that the humanities did not have the answer. Nor was he able to find one anywhere else.

Chapter Two

The Short Fiction

An Early Success

Given the taste of the times, it is not surprising that one of Kees's first published stories should be written in a style heavily reminiscent of Ernest Hemingway. "Saturday Rain" was published in 1935 in *Prairie Schooner* and probably had its origin in a creative-writing class. The first paragraph suggests whom Kees had been reading:

When the train came to a stop, I picked out my bag from the railing above me and said good-bye to the old man with whom I had been talking. He had asked me if I lived in Barker, and I had told him that I had lived there several years before, and that I came back to visit friends on an average of about once a month. "You must have a sweetheart there," the old man said, smiling at me, and fingering his clean, white string tie. I had told him that I did and also that I had been worried about her, as I hadn't heard from her for over a week. He had comforted me by saying something about the occasional slip-ups in the delivery of mail. . . .[1]

The preference for *and* as connective and conjunction (to the exclusion of any other) reminds one of Hemingway, of course, and will be kept up throughout the entire story. The rather melancholy tone is Hemingway's too, already suggesting the painful loss of a lover which will make up the story's theme. The repetition of *and* also gives the story something of the hypnotic effect of a reverie, in which all of the conventions and archetypes associated with a failure in love are brought into play. The rainy, miserable day reinforces the narrator's melancholy; he is embarrassed to see that his girl has taken up with another man; he is forced to spend some time in the company of both of them; he tries to get away and shield his embarrassment and hurt as soon as possible; and he feels obviously inadequate in comparison to his rival. Finally he simply walks away, hurt, but incapable of any response or justification for what has happened to him. The past-tense narration allows the narrator to evoke these experiences as needed, without having to develop individual scenes devoted to minute, naturalistic examinations and behavior. Thus, the most painful scene in the whole story occurs when the narrator is ushered into his unfaithful girl friend's house by her new lover and made to take off his wet outer coat and have some warm tea. This scene is simply condensed into a single paragraph which begins, "From then on, I can't remember exactly how things happened. . . ." But, of course, he remembers the important things, without shifting sympathy to either of the other characters or breaking the overriding melancholy tone. Forty years later the story is still appealing and well-crafted, even if a little too derivative.

But it was not a path he would continue to follow. The Hemingwayesque manner of connecting everything with *and* would go, along with its implication that every event is of equal value in this valueless world. And he would also drop the first-person narration and the freedom it gave him to construct tonal as opposed to scenic effects. More importantly, perhaps, he would also tend to lose any normal sympathy for his characters, not only for characters like the old man in the white string tie at the beginning of "Saturday Rain" but even for his protagonists. Instead, most of Kees's short stories turn out either to be concerned, in the manner of Flaubert and Sinclair Lewis, with a trenchant satire of certain character types or with the depiction of unfortunate victims of economic determinism, creatures bereft of any humanity they might have once had.

While it is next to useless to evaluate an artist in terms of what he did not do, it seems an inescapable conclusion that Kees chose the wrong vehicles for his foray into the short-story form. He was certainly successful in terms of the times: while he never managed to place stories in journals that paid handsomely, he nevertheless managed to publish approximately forty stories in various little magazines over a five- or six-year period. Few beginning writers can expect to do so well. And for annual editions of *Best Short Stories* between 1935 and 1940, the editor, Edward J. O'Brien, chose to single out—though not reprint—

close to a dozen of those stories as being among the best produced in each particular year. In the 1941 edition, O'Brien actually reprinted one of Kees's stories, "The Life of the Mind," and dedicated the whole volume to the virtually unknown Kees. And yet, when we read the stories today, and especially when we read them with the greater accomplishment of Kees's poetry in mind, we cannot help being disappointed. In "Saturday Rain," Kees was able to sustain a mood of melancholy through the tonal and rhythmic control of a first-person flowing style. In most of the other stories, the emphasis invariably shifts to characters clearly dissociated from the author and usually described in the third person. This is Kees's undoing. For, as a satirist, Kees picks targets that are far too easy to satirize, far too dull, boring, or faulty for there to be any justification for elaborate attack. They are self-evidently boring and defective; there is no need for the satirist to keep trying to make a point of it. And, as a naturalist intent upon showing the horrors of the Depression, Kees either picks characters who cannot convince us that they would have more nobility or promise in good times or else tries to make Depression-induced tedium the whole point of the story. Unrelieved tedium can be carried only so far. In short, Kees cannot seem to create characters of sufficient complexity to engage us for very long or to dispel the suspicion that the author is beating a dead horse.

"Mrs. Lutz"

Perhaps one of the weakest stories is "Mrs. Lutz," an effort also published in *Prairie Schooner*. The title character is the middle-aged proprietor of a tea room in a midwestern town, and the story is obviously designed to emphasize what a banal life she leads and what a skewed sense of values she has. Mrs. Lutz, "holding the menus in her puffy hands," is counting the blessings of a good lunch trade when she suddenly notices that the waitress has not given one of the customers an ashtray. The waitress, needless to say, is not to be found at the moment: "That girl! Well, Mrs. Lutz decided, she would just have to take an ashtray to the man herself. She'd just have to do it herself, she guessed."[2] Kees likes to assign such pretentious repetitions of trivial thoughts to his characters' interior monologues. It helps emphasize both the banality of their mental processes and the manner in which they think such problems must be handled. And Mrs. Lutz turns from being banal to meanly vicious when she chews out the waitress and from vicious to venal when she surreptitiously appropriates the quarter tip the customer has left for the waitress. "That would pay for her movie that afternoon. . . . The quarter would just take care of her movie that afternoon," she thinks, with the inevitable repetition.

Of course, Mrs. Lutz is the kind of person one loves to hate, but even the most obnoxious person gains sympathy when being bullied. Perhaps we don't actually come to sympathize with Mrs. Lutz, but we are left wondering why Kees has chosen to train such big guns on such an insignificant target. A middle-aged woman, probably widowed, forced to earn a living by operating a tea room, is hardly the best example of what is wrong with Depression-era civilization, no matter how distressing her faults might be. And because she really is responsible for so few of the world's ills, the reader is left in the very peculiar position of not knowing what he could possibly do to make the world safe from the Mrs. Lutzes and hardly convinced that it would make much difference even if he had (and exercised) such knowledge.

"So Cold Outside"

"So Cold Outside" is a slightly more complex version of "Mrs. Lutz" which basically sticks to the same kind of unsympathetic exploration of the midwestern mind. It is set in a department store on a freezing wintry day and is seen mostly through the consciousness of George W. Spencer, a shoe clerk, and Lela Murcheson, who works in ladies' wear. The weather is bad enough to keep customers away, and the store's employees are forced to spend long, boring hours waiting for closing time. Fortunately, they also have a scapegoat, someone upon whom to channel their frustrations over the slow business and horrible weather. It is a woman, obviously penniless and perhaps homeless, who has ducked into the store to avoid the rigors of the freezing weather. Soon the employees notice her.

"Maybe she's a shoplifter," George said.
"That's just what I've been thinking."

"They better keep an eye on her."

"Well, I'll bet you're right about that, George," Lela said. "It wouldn't surprise me if she was a shoplifter." (275)[3]

The banality and smugness of the conversation is self-evident, but in another stretch of dialogue Kees goes further to suggest how solipsistic his characters are. Lela and another salesgirl talk about the weather without either ever entering the world of the other. The other girl can chatter about nothing but the trouble her husband had starting the car; Lela can only repeat how she had almost frozen coming to work. George, the only character who even entertains any thoughts about where the old woman could go once she's been thrown out of the store, quickly dismisses such speculations. "But hell, that was one of those things that happened, and it sure wasn't any concern of his" (282). Lela again shows the same sort of solipsistic absorption as she converts her resentment of the old woman into resentment of her boy friend.

The more she thought about it, the madder she got. It just made her boil. And she was beginning to get pretty irritated about Dale not calling her up. . . . She loved him so, and how did he repay her love? How?

And the trivial nature of Lela's chain of thought continues as she thinks of eating lunch, wishes her boy friend would have lunch with her, and then bounds off into further resentment when she realizes he won't.

Kees, in other words, has done a good job of showing how the characters lack basic human sympathy and the ability to break out of their own petty concerns. But once again he has locked himself into a corner, best exemplified when George thinks about Little Orphan Annie:

That was one of the best comics going, exciting and sort of real, too. George felt sorry for Daddy Warbucks: there he had built up a great business, a business to benefit humanity, and what happened to him? A bunch of radicals and malcontents had gone to work and stirred up trouble for him. (281)

More than he would like to admit in these stories, I suspect, Kees was simply declaring himself to be alienated from everyone. The old, impoverished woman is only seen from a distance;

we feel sorry for the injustice done to her but hardly get a
chance to identify with her feelings. The rest of the characters
are unsympathetic. If Daddy Warbucks's world is not the world
of the future, where is a better world to come from? Despite
hints of a fashionable radicalism, neither here nor in any of
his other stories does Kees ever produce any viable social alternative or even a positive pole for satire.

"The Life of the Mind"

A good example of both the strengths and weaknesses of
Kees's satirical bent is "The Life of the Mind," the short story
that O'Brien chose to include in the 1941 edition of *Best Short
Stories,* dedicated to Kees. The trenchant irony begins with the
title, since the protagonist, a college English professor, has apparently never had a real life of the mind. Certainly in his later
days he has become the most reprehensible of college teachers—
the friend of the football players. The story, which takes place
during one day of his life, shows him getting far more upset
over an interview with a high-principled young instructor who
refuses to change a player's failing grade than over the death
of his wife in a mental asylum. Kees's placing of the protagonist
beyond the pale of our sympathy is accomplished in the first
four sentences: "Too many things were weighing on Dr. Peate's
mind. There was his wife, for one thing. He did not know
whether she was dead or alive. He hoped she was dead" (161).[4]
By the end of the story she is dead; and he, of course, is moved
only by the possible cost of the funeral. This lack of response
is typical of his stunted emotional life: he had never really loved
his wife; and, in perhaps the story's most successfully understated
moments, we perceive that he is really a latent homosexual
with a sort of locker-room admiration for the university's football
team. Mrs. Peate "had been extravagant, silly, and too insatiable
in a certain way for Dr. Peate, whose hiking activities seemed
to take a lot out of him" (162). That she was extravagant and
silly is not just Dr. Peate's point of view; it is clearly shared
by the narrator as well. She is, in other words, simply another
example of the inanity of modern life. In fact, the only admirable
character in the short story is Milstein, the young professor
who refuses to change the football player's grade. But Milstein

does not really figure in the story at all, except as a foil for Dr. Peate, and his name is obviously chosen to allow Kees to demonstrate that Peate is something of an anti-Semite as well. In one of the more genuinely humorous passages, Peate's encounter with the Jewish Milstein makes him think of Jews in general:

They had never had any luck with Jews, he reflected. One of them had written proletarian poems. They had got rid of him in a hurry. Another, Mr. Kauffman, they had discovered after he had gone on to Harvard, had been living with a blonde who worked as a typist for the Federal Housing Authority. They had been quite open about it. A lot of people had known. The blonde had been a good-looker too. (166)

The last sentence shows how Kees could lose control of his diction. "Good-looker" is not the type of slang a college English professor, no matter how moronic, is likely to use; and the judgment itself is inconsistent with the pervasive hints of Dr. Peate's woman-hating homosexuality.

The story ends with Dr. Peate thinking "how silly he has been, allowing himself to get so worked up by a person like Milstein. There were lots of ways to fix him" (172–73). Nothing in the story contradicts this reassurance. We are forced to assume that Dr. Peate does indeed have the clout to coerce Milstein or override his grade. Such an ending is more or less typical of Kees's satiric fictions. Peate may be the satiric butt of the story, but he in no way feels it and in no way gets any sort of comeuppance at the end. His dull and mindless reign over the academic destiny of the football team will continue. In short, Kees's fictions are not simply told by a superior moralist but a profoundly alienated one, pessimistic about any real reform or change.

Such pessimism does not seem forced and may explain the lack of liveliness—or even misguided liveliness—on the part of Kees's protagonist. Such people are simply too dreadful for the writer to want to give them any attractive features, including the attraction of energy. Peate's admiration for the muscular bodies of young athletes (he even accompanies them on out-of-town trips on occasion) gives him no real life of the spirit, and his days are spent in the dreary confines of the university and his bachelor's hotel room. But if the author's pessimism does not seem forced, it does seem terribly "stuck-up" on occasion. Our sense of English syntax and the conventions of fiction tell us that when a narrator says, "He would go home and take a bracing cold shower and drink a glass of carrot juice" (171), the subject of the sentence is being satirized. And the self-abnegation implicit in cold showers and carrot juice (especially in place of an evening meal) does tend to deflate a character. But what are we to make of some of the details? For example, we are told "He had special arch-preservers fitted into all of his shoes. The arch-preservers dated from his first days in the hiking club." If these details are simply "realistic" or "naturalistic" then they are mere padding—they do nothing to advance the story. But Kees probably means them as a put-down. But why should wearing arch supports be the occasion for snobbish condescension? In short, throughout Kees's work of this sort, one again and again hears the almost conspiratorial voice of the cultivated midwestern intellectual, so appalled by the level of taste and sensibility around and so convinced of his own isolation that he loses all sense of the distinction between substance and accident, between pointing out a foible and merely recording a difference. We understand from the very beginning, thanks to such details, that the narrator is far superior in taste and sensibility and that the protagonist is impervious to good sense or good taste. But such a dichotomy, in the absence of some tonal or metaphoric magic which Kees did not bring, does not produce a very exciting story. Nevertheless, Kees wrote many in this mode.

"Three Pretty Nifty Green Suits"

More heavily plotted is "Three Pretty Nifty Green Suits," set, like "So Cold Outside," in a department store. Howard Wigmore, a salesman, gets a shipment of three green suits, which everyone agrees are pretty nifty. He puts the size thirty-six in the window and the other two on the racks. Before the day is over, he has sold all three of them. The first he sells to Bill Cummings, a local inhabitant, who reveals that he is leaving for California. The second he sells to a traveling musician, who buys it only on condition that it be altered within the hour so he can leave town on schedule. This sets the scene for the sale of the third suit to Arn Cheatham, something of the town bully, around whom Howard always feels uncomfortable. Arn buys the suit only on one condition: it must be the only one of its kind in town. Remembering that Bill has said he is going to California, Howard tells Arn about the other two sales. Arn buys the suit and Howard goes home a happy man, thinking about his commissions.

But now the story takes a twist and reveals more plotting than is usual for Kees. Arn reappears the next day and grabs Howard by the lapels and starts sputtering about being tricked. It turns out he had seen Bill the night before and found out Bill's trip to California is off. In his not-too-bright way, Arn holds Howard responsible. But now another salesman comes up, finds out what is going on, and after some teasing questions ("What time did you see Bill?") reveals that later that evening Bill was in a terrible car crash. He is not expected to live. Of course, this is the moment Kees has been building toward, the moment where the banality of the men's response to the news will be apparent. In his bovine stupidity, Arn can only repeat the details of the accident, murmur "that's tough," and apologize to Howard for his behavior. Howard, paradoxically, feels his intimidated heart starting to beat again. Soon, "things would be all right":

And then Arn would leave and Howard would be able to go to the back room and re-order on the green suits for some possible out-of-town trade. Still, on second thought, he wasn't so sure. He looked at Arn and decided it might be better not to. (300)[5]

Again, it is hard to know exactly what Kees intends here. One suspects that he is trying to satirize the men's lack of significant—and felt—response to the imminent death of someone they all know. But, in fact, Kees's psychology works so well that the effect is more realistic than satiric: men normally have trouble finding words or gestures capable of dealing with death. Nevertheless, with its variation on the theme of the small-town bully chastised, the story does have some good touches. And

it is also notable for one almost Gogolesque touch when Howard
goes home the night after selling the three suits to have a most
delicious dream. In it, he was wearing

a double-breasted green suit with a huge price tag on it, and he was
walking in a green meadow and people were pointing at him and
saying, "There goes Howard Wigmore. That's Howard Wigmore;
he's a big shot around here, all right." (297)

But there is no real sympathy for Howard or for the aspirations
of a men's suit salesman, and the story ends with Howard making
one of the repetitious remarks we have seen Kees use before
to indicate a character's obtuseness.

"A Walk Home"

"A Walk Home" is probably the best example of a story
that Kees could just as easily have turned into a far more sympathetic treatment of his protagonist. In fact, one is uncomfortably
aware at times of the kind of sadistic urge that seems to vitiate
several of his stories. Perhaps the mistake starts with Kees's
selection of a protagonist and with the nature of the plot's conflict. Mr. Chalmers has a glass eye, and the story revolves around
his losing the eye and then recovering it. His physical handicap
does not seem to be the source of any vile character traits which
might justify a satirical treatment of him; he is simply one of
Kees's dull-minded and imperceptive protagonists.

Mr. Chalmers goes to the movies wearing his new glass eye,
which begins to give him a lot of pain. He decides to put up
with the pain until he gets back to his rooming house, in order
to save the embarrassment of removing it in public. On his
way out, he thinks about the theater's air conditioning in a
way that reveals he is as obtusely paranoid as some of Kees's
other characters.

He reflected that this airconditioning [sic] was a great thing, all right.
A great thing. And somebody was making a barrel of money out of
it, you bet. Yes sir. He wished that he could get in on a good thing
like that, but it was always the other fellow who got the breaks. (167)[6]

But the pain becomes too intense during his walk home. He
stops to remove the eye and drops it through a sidewalk grating.

Although embarrassed to do so, he is finally forced to seek help from a passerby who turns out to be a true samaritan. But this example of human cooperation simply serves Kees as an occasion to reproduce some slightly inane, slightly understated masculine banter ("It wasn't nothing at all." "Don't mention it.") and the short story closes with Kees once again attempting to emphasize Mr. Chalmers's impotent rage at the way the world treats him.

> Tomorrow he would certainly tell that Shearer [the oculist] a thing or two. Shearer had better not get the idea that he could get by with that sort of stuff. Mr. Chalmers would certainly tell him where to get off, don't think he wouldn't. (170)

Needless to say, a twist of perspective allowing Mr. Chalmers to be bathed in sentimental humanism of the 1930s would not help this story, either. But left the way it is, the reader can only wonder why Kees really wanted to pick on a man with one eye.

"Applause"

The question of sympathy for the protagonist is a little more perplexing in "Applause." Ira Conlee could have come straight out of Sinclair Lewis. A typical small-town, lower-middle-class booster, he has finally finagled a chance to hear his hero, the great Walter F. Hoke, deliver one of his inspirational messages. Mr. Hoke, whom Kees makes the author of *Life's What You Make It* and *Making A Go Of Living,* is, of course, the typical exponent of positive thinking, a sort of respectable con artist still prevalent in some circles of American life. And Ira Conlee is extra proud that he is going to hear Mr. Hoke because "he, Ira Conlee, had been the one responsible for Walter F. Hoke's coming here to speak this evening" (128).[7] It seems that when Ira heard that the Junior League was planning a lecture series, he called Lillian Jennings right away and suggested Hoke.

So Ira gathers up his copies of Hoke's books—to be autographed afterwards—and heads with his wife for the auditorium. Hoke turns out to be everything Ira had hoped he would be. Only one thing spoils the evening. The man in front of Ira

refuses to applaud. Ira grows more and more irate and finally
leans over and asks the man, "What's the matter with you anyway, buddy?" The man does not answer, he simply turns his
head and looks at Ira. After several further embarrassing ex-
changes, the talk ends and, of course, the man stands up and
reveals that he is missing an arm.

So much for the comeuppance of a booster like Ira Conlee.
But it is precisely here that Kees either loses control or else
deliberately diverts our sympathy to Ira. It is hard to tell which.
Ira looks away from the empty sleeve, "blood rushing to his
face," and feeling a "horrible sinking in his stomach":

> The man was gone. Conlee felt powerless, as though he would never
> be able to move again. People crowded the narrow aisles, their voices
> growing, buzzing in the room, and he felt that all of them were staring
> at him. The books by Walter Hoke had fallen to the floor, and he
> looked at them stupidly.
> His wife's voice, when it came, was cold and distant. "Come on,
> Ira," she said. (131)

The wife's reaction is the final indignity, and her turning on
her husband in his embarrassment almost guarantees our sympathy. But the fundamental point is that Ira is embarrassed. A
genuine booster would find some way to bluster his way out
of the situation—Ira is genuinely shaken. Thus the real question
is how are we to mesh the first part of the story, where Ira is
obviously being held up to ridicule as a type of midwestern
Boobus Americanus, with the end where Ira is shown to be capable
of being shamed. If Ira were really capable of such feeling upon
such a relatively mild pretext, then the original lampooning
was unfair. It is hard to see how any reconciliation will really
work. As suggested earlier, Kees probably simply lost control
of the reader's sympathy.

"Gents 50¢; Ladies 25¢"

But there is one satirical story where Kees does want to generate sympathy for the main character. "Gents 50¢; Ladies 25¢"
could be entitled "Madame Bovary in Nebraska." Like Flaubert's Emma Bovary, Dorajean Meltzer is a romantically inclined

young woman who finds herself trapped in a decidedly realistic and dreary world. Dorajean sells tickets to a dance hall; and while she sits in her booth, making change for drunks and other local riffraff, her fantasy life keeps her warm:

> She was Ann Harding now, glorious blond Ann, and she didn't have crooked teeth or a nose that was too pointed. She was Ann Harding, and Ronald Colman was just about to ask her to go away with him in his Packard convertible. "I belong to you alone, Ronald," Dorajean Meltzer whispered to herself. "We are one forever and a day." (69)[8]

When she is not thinking of Ronald Colman and projecting herself into the latest Hollywood movie she has seen, she is thinking about the cute bass player in the band, who she is sure is far more suave and polished than Art, her actual boyfriend. Art works at the local flour mill and has "flour in his ears and in the little wrinkles around his eyes. Art [smells] of flour" (70).

But even though Dorajean's fantasy life is satirized, it is also a sign that she possesses something that Kees's less sympathetic characters never do. She is capable of responding to her environment in a sensitive way, capable of projecting her own future within that environment. It is this last ability that brings about the crisis at the heart of the story. Often three women, "young, but thin and undernourished," come up to the dance hall and try to peer past Dorajean's booth at the dancers. They compose a tableau to be found in hundreds of Depression-era photographs. They wear "cheap print dresses," one is carrying a baby, and all are terribly old before their time.

Dorajean knows who these creatures are. Their husbands work the nightshift at a local factory, so they are poor but not destitute and simply bored with their evenings rather than perpetually unhoused. But they always make her uncomfortable, and tonight she realizes why:

> Looking at the three women, Dorajean began to think that they were only a few years older than she was, five or six or seven years, perhaps, and already they were thin and unattractive and cross looking. They had just let themselves go, she told herself. (70)

But Dorajean knows this isn't so. The grind of poverty and childbearing had done the same thing to her mother and would do it to her. In a frightening moment, she sees her own future, the almost immediate future, in the eyes of those women. And she also sees no way out. She can avoid it perhaps by not marrying Art, but then she would simply have to stay in a menial job like ticket-selling for the rest of her days. The depressing and inevitable future of the Midwest working class sinks into her. There will be no Ronald Colmans for her. Suddenly she feels what amounts to the first stage of a nervous breakdown coming on. The music no longer impresses her; the bass player is no longer cute; nothing seems to have value for her, including her fantasies, which she now knows will never come true. And she keeps seeing herself "in a dirty cotton house dress with her skin stretched tightly over the bones of her face, with her mouth drawn and hard" (72).

The rest of the story is less well handled. Art shows up in his car, oblivious, of course, of Dorajean's crisis. There are so many conflicting impulses in her head (to scream, to laugh, to cry) that she can only try to escape them. "I want to go fast," she tells Art, "I want to go fast in the car." She tries to explain what's wrong but cannot, and soon Art is trying to tell a story about something that happened at the mill. But Dorajean, looking forward to the fast ride to make her forget, isn't even listening.

The problem with the ending is that racing down the highway in the middle of the night is a far more delicious escape—as seen in the movies—than Dorajean will ever really achieve. Kees's point is valid enough: there is no real solution. But it is somewhat undercut by the romantic possibilities of the image of speed.

"The Sign Painters"

"The Sign Painters" is more unabashed social protest. Mac, the protagonist, and Gene, his business partner and natural antagonist, are really no different from the characters we have seen Kees handle so disdainfully in his satiric stories, but at least Mac's shortcomings are rationalized in economic terms.

To begin with, the two men are former competitors, forced to combine their sign-painting business because of the Depression. Unlike the satiric stories, the whole work is studded with reminders of bad times. The men have not had any work in a week; they are quite penniless. A fellow shopkeeper wanders into the story to lament that his son had hitchhiked to Kansas City in search of a job, only to find it was already taken. The man's lament is stoical—not much else could really be expected. The only consolation both Mac and the father can find, ironically, is that neither is on relief or being evicted like another family they know of.

Indeed family responsibilities are one thing that help fuel the antagonism Mac feels for Gene. Having extra mouths to feed is a special burden during hard times:

> The way Gene took things, so damned easy. When they were out of work, as they were so often, Mac would feel restless and moody and angry at the world, and it didn't help a hell of a lot when Gene acted so damned easy-going. "We'll get by," Gene would say. Yeh, it was OK to talk like that when you were single like Gene; but, say, it was an altogether different story when you had a wife and a kid to feed.[9]

Gene's easy-going manner is not entirely so benign, however. He loves to taunt Mac at just the wrong times, loves to drive Mac livid by holding back on what meager amounts of good news there are. The action of the story, in fact, revolves around Gene's taking a phone call and arranging for the first job the men have had all week. Mac is dying for the details; Gene repeatedly taunts him with "wouldn't you like to know?" Gene is at best frozen into a permanent adolescence, and we are not surprised when Mac finally slugs him.

But Kees has not handled the ending of the story very well. Before being hit, Gene actually does let Mac in on the details of the job. The Chamber of Commerce wants the men to paint four new signs to place out on the highways leading into the town. The message on the signs is bitterly ironic, as Gene admits when he shows the copy to Mac: "PROSPERITY HAS RETURNED TO WESTON. THE WESTON CHAMBER OF COMMERCE. 8000 FRIENDLY PEOPLE WELCOME YOU." "Ain't that a laugh?" Gene insists. Whereupon Mac, having had altogether too much for one day, becomes violent. The problem, of course, is that Kees has created an innocent victim. Gene's juvenile behavior would have made Mac's reaction somewhat plausible and defensible earlier in the story. But here Mac and Gene's points of view coincide, and Gene is just as aware of the absurdity of the taste-less boosterism as Mac is. Kees is doubtless aiming for psycholog-ical validity, but it would have been more believable if Mac had rammed his fist into the wall to demonstrate how impotent a small-town sign painter is when caught up in a worldwide economic collapse.

"A Man To Help"

That impotence is better revealed in "A Man To Help" where there is no violent action and, indeed, not much action at all. Max, an unemployed male of indeterminate age, catches a street-car to go see about a job advertised in the paper. When he gets there, the job (as dishwasher) has already been taken. He falls into conversation with an older German who tells him that things are tough here but even tougher in Germany and that the most extraordinary thing he discovered when he first came to New York was chewing gum. Finally, they separate and Max buys a newspaper, looks at the help-wanted column, finds another possibility, and waits for the streetcar to take him across town once again.

Such a plot, or line of action perhaps, is ideal for describing the inability of the character to alter his predicament. Max knows there are no jobs, and Kees has inserted a number of hints that Max is being affected by this knowledge. Still, he persists; but one is left with the suspicion that his fatalism is catching up with him, that soon the streetcar rides in pursuit of jobs will stop altogether and he will become another victim of hope-lessness.

"I Should Worry"

In one of his letters to James Laughlin (2 October 1938), Kees mentions a story that he has had a hard time placing because of its subject matter. He does not mention the title, but evidence suggests that he is talking about "I Should Worry," one of two stories by Kees that Laughlin published in *New Directions*. The story's subject matter hardly seems that objectionable today, but it is a trenchant example of the thesis that bad times can lead people to actions they would otherwise find unconscionable, and it is the closest Kees comes to writing a story of "degradation" on the order of Erskine Caldwell or some of the other southern writers of the time.

"I Should Worry," however, is firmly set in the Midwest. Like Mac in "The Sign Painters," Arch Boyle runs a small and unsuccessful business, a second-hand auto-parts shop. And also like Mac, Arch Boyle has a family, or at least a deaf and dumb sister to take care of. But if the grubby surface of Depression-era poverty is the same, very little else is. Kees has embarked on a far more ambitious project here, and it is easy to see why some editors would feel frustrated by their inability to publish the story. (Kees claims Robert Penn Warren was one such editor.) Arch Boyle is someone beaten down by the Depression; but unlike Kees's other heroes, he is capable of articulating his rage and his angst. His sister is not as successful a creation because her behavior suggests mental retardation—promiscuous sexual relations seem to be the only thing she thinks of—but Kees tries to suggest that her amorality is the psychic reaction to the same forces that are driving Arch down.

The story begins with a too-long encounter between Arch and his antagonist, who runs a radio repair shop across the street and blasts music through a loud speaker too loud for Arch's taste. Obviously this encounter is designed to set the stage for the tedium that is Arch's life and frustration, but it also leaves us completely unprepared for the appearance of Arch's sister. Betty Lou comes downstairs into the shop from their living quarters, "a green knit dress stretched tight over her body." She also has a broken arm, the product of a mysterious tryst the week before. Arch, all-around handyman that he is, set the arm himself but could never get Betty Lou to indicate how it had happened. The suspected sexual violence, while obviously making her unhappy, has apparently not cooled her nymphomania. Every time Kees describes her it is in terms of a too tightly dressed, too made-up, overly obvious sexual creature.

"If my mother and the old man had lived," Arch thinks, maybe his sister would have turned out differently (108).[10] Given the present situation, however, he does not see any way to change her sexual habits. And he has problems of his own.

He yearns for some gin to take his mind off things—even fanta-
sizes that he will dig up some dirt on the landlord so he can
get his rent money back to buy booze with. Why he wants
the gin becomes obvious in his interior monologue:

Maybe some people have lives that make sense, he thought. Maybe
some of them do things that make some difference, maybe for some
of them it goes some place and has some meaning. More meaning
than getting up in the hot or the cold morning, it doesn't make any
difference, and putting on a pair of dirty socks and clothes that you
wore yesterday and eating breakfast with a sister that can't hear you
or speak to you. And all of the time you're wondering what's going
on in her mind. And then you go down to the shop and wait on
customers, if you're lucky enough to have any, and then by the time
night comes around you toss a slug of gin inside of you and after
you're good and drunk you fall into bed dog-tired and feel it spinning
around beneath you and hear the street cars rumbling by in the dark
and your head feeling like a bomb about to explode. (108)

Such awareness does not stop him from performing the action
which must have shocked several prospective editors. A customer comes into the shop to buy a ten-cent item, and Arch,
aware of his destitution and his craving for a shot of gin, notices
the man staring at Betty Lou. "I've done it before," Arch thinks,
"but never when she's had a broken arm" (110). Nevertheless
he prostitutes his sister, haggling with the man until he gets
$1.75 in exchange for a quick trip upstairs with Betty Lou.
Arch makes $1.85 for the whole day, saves the dollar for grocer-
ies and goes out to get drunk on the eighty-five cents as his
sister, who seems happy enough about the arrangement, heads
upstairs with the man.

Arch is not quite so happy, of course. His hesitation to prosti-
tute his sister while her arm is broken suggests some general
moral revulsion, and at the end of the story, he is still lamenting
the fact the Betty Lou is the way she is:

I should worry about her. Because that's all she knows. Because it's
been that way ever since the two of them [i.e., his parents] stuffed
the doors of the living room with newspapers and turned on the
gas and waited there, sitting in the chairs by the window, with that
slow hissing all around them. And the smell getting stronger all the

time. Because that's the way it's been ever since then with her. I tried to stop her too many times and then I gave up. (112)

And he gives up on himself as well, turning off his thoughts and heading for the bar and the gin. The cause of his parents' suicide is never given, but it is obvious that it traumatized Betty Lou; and, along with the sour economic conditions, Betty Lou's aberrations are more than Arch can successfully cope with. Yet he has not become a moral cipher or an unfeeling lout like characters in many of Kees's other stories. His selling of his sister has no further adverse effect on her—she would do it for free and often does, apparently—but it hurts him and makes him even more embittered against his circumstances. And he continues to think he should be concerned about her though he is impotent to change her ways. Certainly of all Kees's attempts to treat the effects of the Depression sympathetically, "I Should Worry" is the most effective.

"This Is Home"

Some stories, while perhaps not dropping either the social satire or economic determinism completely, seem to treat the material in a more detached, objective way. In other words, some of the stories seem to be best grouped under the term "slice of life." "Slice of life" is usually taken to mean a story in which plot is not critical and the author is more interested in an objective description of either scenic backgrounds or psychological states. Oddly enough, one of the best examples of this type is a story whose overt subject matter is every bit as salacious as that of "I Should Worry." But Kees apparently had no trouble finding a publisher for "This Is Home." It appeared in a little magazine called *Manuscript* in the spring of 1936. Perhaps the magazine was a little more daring than most; perhaps Kees simply manages to be especially discreet in dealing with the subject. Simply told, the story is about a sailor alone on leave in the city who is picked up by a man who offers to take him home to have a beer and to meet his "wife and kid." "Wife and kid" convinces Banning, the sailor, that the man is not a homosexual; and, besides, the man also insists that he has a brother in the navy, that entertaining other sailors helps him keep in "touch" with his brother. What the man is actually doing, however, is procuring the unsuspecting Banning as a sexual partner for his wife, a woman of beauty and apparently normal appetites. As far as one can tell, it is the husband's impotence that occasions these forays for unattached males. There is a modicum of suspense: Banning and the reader are deceived until the last minute when, sufficiently full of beer, he discovers Eve (the woman's name) lying naked in bed and makes love to her. Afterwards, Eve's husband drives him back to where he had originally been picked up. The story ends with Banning feeling sorry for the husband and trying to express it. But Banning cannot, and the man does not want to hear it anyway. And so they part, the husband crying to himself, Banning thinking, "The poor devil."

What is remarkable here is that while the husband is described as "weak" and beaten down, he is neither satirized nor made out to be a victim of the Depression. And Banning is simply a sailor of moderate intelligence who wanders into a bizarre experience. The emphasis, in other words, is more on the psychology of the situation than is usual in Kees's stories.

"Downward and Away"

Much the same could be said for "Downward and Away" which reminds one of Hemingway's "The Killers" and is an attempt to create a drama out of an overhead conversation in a restaurant. The story opens with a Hemingwayesque description of a man's attempt to eat a ham sandwich:

From time to time he would open the sandwich and pick up the catsup bottle and put a little catsup between the slices of bread. Then he would close up the sandwich again and eat until he needed some more catsup.[11]

As in Hemingway, there are no "markers" in this passage to indicate whether the author takes this action to be significant or trivial. But the focus soon shifts to a couple drinking coffee in one of the booths, and their conversation is decidedly mysterious. They are waiting for a third person to appear who is apparently bringing them something. We never know who he is or what he is bringing, but we can see that the couple is very tense and anxious—obviously they are awaiting something (or someone) of grave importance. They reminisce about happier times in Seattle, wish they were there now, and finally leave the restaurant when it becomes clear that they have been stood up. Only one bit of dialogue gives any suggestion about why the visit is so important:

"My God, Harry," the girl went on rapidly. "If we don't get it from him you know what'll happen to us, you know what they'll do to us—"

"Yeh," he said, looking down at the floor.

Presumably they are in the position of having welshed on a deal with some unsavory characters who do not take such renegings lightly. But that is all we learn, and the story ends up giving us a "slice of life" depicting two worried individuals, and then frames it in a cheap restaurant. Perhaps for greater ironic effect, the waitress points out their behavior to another customer who, of course, is more interested in the trajectory of the cap off his latest bottle of beer. In its desperation and grubbiness, in the inability of its main characters to remedy their situation, "Downward and Away" hints at economic determinism, but the hints are very weak.

"The Ceremony"

"The Ceremony" is much the same in its casual evocation of economic realities, though the main characters more closely resemble the protagonists of the satiric short stories. Floyd Hollenbeck, the owner of a construction company, receives a call from his foreman, telling him that he had better get out to the construction site right away. Hollenbeck is an obviously insensitive Middle American, and his grumbling does nothing to endear him to us. When he arrives at the site where his company is erecting a barbecue stand, he finds out that the two-man crew is refusing to work any further because they have dug up a "petrified" Indian. In his obtuse way, Hollenbeck forces the men to consider their stomachs before any reverence for or superstitious fears of the dead. As the men—having been threatened with being blacklisted forever—break up the petrified corpse with their sledge hammers, Floyd cracks a joke and then repeats it. "The vanishing American," Hollenbeck says. "Get it?" The point is indeed gotten, and Floyd is very happy with himself. "Hollenbeck couldn't get over how funny it was. He laughed harder. The vanishing American. And it had come to him just like that. Without thinking about it at all."[12] This weak jest will have to do, despite the story's title, in place of any ceremony for the long-dead Indian, and this jibe at Floyd's obtuseness will have to serve as pretty much the whole point of the story, since Kees passes up the opportunity to explore the men's reluctance to desecrate the Indian remains or to linger for more than a line or two over Floyd's feelings when he actually touches the flesh made stone.

More Experimental Stories

Of course, some works will not be neatly pigeonholed into either social satire, economic determinism, or "slice of life." "Saturday Rain" was such a work, and so are three others: "Escape in Autumn," "Four Stories," and "The Evening of the Fourth of July." All have in common the attempt to break the realistic constraints under which the other short stories function.

"Escape in Autumn," however, is by no means one of Kees's better stories. Published in the *Windsor Quarterly* in 1935, it is most likely a class exercise, written to assignment. The tone is certainly not identifiable with any of Kees's other efforts. It is in essence a fable. A man with a physically repulsive cancer on the side of his face finds his loneliness relieved by a chance encounter with a blind beggar. Obviously the blind man will not be put off because of the other man's visual disfigurement; and furthermore, the beggar's blindness gives the man with a cancer a chance to fantasize. When the blind beggar asks the man what he looks like, the man with a cancer gives a glowing description of his "fine, smooth skin." They part but agree to meet again the next day, and the man is as happy as he has ever remembered being. This short work (under 1000 words) certainly does not try to be sentimental, but it is hard to see

exactly what else it is trying to do. Kees allows himself to forget
that the blind "see" with their hands and that the blind man
would doubtless want to touch such excellent "smooth skin,"
but then the whole thing is pretty unbelievable in psychological
terms. Otherwise, the fable is more notable for the absence
of the urge to satirize and to blame everything on the Depression.

"Four Stories" is something of an anthology. There are four
different short stories (perhaps five hundred words each) numbered and titled separately. In them Kees seems to be interested
in the absurdity of language and situation that inheres in the
universe rather than in one deficient, satirized character. This
observation is advanced with caution, since at best what is being
noted is merely a tendency, and a half-hearted one, at that.
But since the same interest was to show up again and again in
his poetry, perhaps we are not entirely out of line in seeing a
glimmer of it in these short fictions.

For example, the first story, "Zuni Street Evenings," concerns
a couple with intellectual pretensions (their reading matter includes Clarence Darrow's autobiography and Charles Beard's
Rise of American Civilization). Yet their life seems full of incongru-
ities. He worries about the way his toenails are clipped; they
play a desultory little game with his best necktie; and they go
to bed after she points out her "strawberry festival"—that is,
a hive on her lip caused by eating berries at supper. "Maybe
you ought to quit eating them," he says. "The strawberries."[13]
It is the lack of the heavy-handed satirical techniques that makes
one think that Kees is concentrating more on life's absurdities
and genuine problems of communication rather than on his
characters' deficiencies in this first story.

In the next, "To the Traveller on the Heights Comes Faintly,"
there is a more overt contrast between reality and fantasy, as
a man reads a *National Geographic* description of the faraway
city of Fez and then has to step out into the cold reality of an
American wintry day. None of the warmth of Fez goes with
him, unfortunately.

The third story, "Big Improvement," comes closest to satire,
perhaps; but the main character, Mr. Chisholm, is certainly de-
luded. He is also an excellent craftsman (a sign painter, again)
whose painstaking work is the pride of his wife. But what he

painstakingly applies his paint and brush to is the tritest of signs
for his vacation cabin: "Our Blue Heaven." He sees nothing
tasteless about either his own sign or the wording of his neighbor's ("Dew-Cum-In") but he is extremely contemptuous of
the lack of artistic pride that made the neighbor do such a lousy
job of it. Mr. Chisholm retires with all the serenity of a Hemingway hero who has done something neat and clean and good.
And only we see the absurdity of a world where such dedication
and talent can be devoted to such inane trivia.

The final story, "Two Young Men Wearing Hard Straw Hats
and Summer Wash Suits" is both more satiric and yet still darkly
humorous. The two young men are discussing a third who has
met with serious misfortune and disfigurement. For a few moments their discussion is serious and somber. But mankind cannot stand too much reality, and soon they are back trading
stock jibes at one another, keeping up their roles as sharp and
worldly young studs and using language to insulate themselves
from the world's unpleasantness.

"The Evening of the Fourth of July"

Published, like "I Should Worry," in *New Directions,* an annual
devoted to the avant-garde and featuring some of the most prom-
ising new writers, "The Evening of the Fourth of July," seems
to be not only one of Kees's last attempts at short fiction, but
also his finest. Many of the features found here for the first
time in his fiction will be staples of his poetry. The story, for
example, which revolves around a character named McGoin,
is set in a metropolitan wasteland, not the customary Midwest;
and it has the logic of a nightmare more than that of a piece
of economic realism. Kees had obviously been reading T. S.
Eliot and the surrealist poets, had probably been noticing German expressionist paintings and perhaps films, and may have
been familiar with the Nighttown section of Joyce's *Ulysses.*

Very near the beginning, for example, Kees includes a catalog
of horrific and absurd items McGoin has gleaned from reading
the morning newspaper:

A notorious Continental pervert was being feted in New York. A
captain of industry predicted better times and announced a thirty-

five per cent wage cut. There was a picture of him making the announcement. He had a flower in his button-hole. A ravishingly beautiful Hollywood star was to undergo a dangerous rectal operation at Mother of Christ Memorial Hospital. There were brief accounts of various murders, rapes, swindles, divorces, wars, poisonings, accidents, and beatings, and an illustrated feature of an interesting child-torture case, in which the torturer claimed to have employed his razor-blades and red-hot irons to bring a consciousness of Divine Love to his youthful victims.[14]

Even by itself, this catalog indicates that Kees had found something far more important than the selfish, unsympathetic concerns of a Nebraska widow to occupy his fiction. He had found not just a provincial society but a whole world which did not make sense.

The story seems to be set over a Fourth of July holiday in the near future, when civilization has finally collapsed and Yeats's worst fears about the apocalyptic anarchy of "The Second Coming" have come true. McGoin works as a night watchman in a factory that makes gas masks, a sorely needed item in such a world. Explosions are everywhere; all human behavior has become either pointless or ironic, and McGoin finds it impossible to sleep during the day and to find any meaningful activity to engage in as he wanders through the nightmare landscape. He meets children who throw explosives at him, troops of teenage girls in khaki uniforms marching through the streets, placards reading "BUTCHER OUR ENEMIES!" and a daffy woman who defends the murderous activities of the children: "I'd think you'd have some consideration for the innocent pleasures of tiny children on such a happy holiday!" (58). Later, he watches mysterious figures in blue police uniforms mow down a group of strikers without anyone objecting. The strikers, moments before, have been listening to strange guttural sounds—apparently meant to be inflammatory rhetoric—coming out of ear-shaped amplifiers.

And, as in Eliot's *Waste Land,* the more articulate elements of society lead lives equally pointless. McGoin ducks into a bar to be with friends, and their brittle chatter immediately shows their vacuity.

"Jackson has the crabs," said Engblom.
"I know."
"Takes it well, doesn't he?"

* * * * * * * * * * *

"You know, Vernon, my wife has a lot of integrity," Quayhagen
observed.
"Are you living with her again?"
"She left me Thursday. . . ." (61–63)

Attempts at real communication come to nothing, but the world
still has professional do-gooders, including a Miss Ridpath, who
is full of high sentences about adult education and thinks "Spen-
gler is such fun." Fortunately there is still enough energy left
in this declining world to send Miss Ridpath off to her proper
reward:

She rose, unable to contain herself, tremendously enthused, her face
flushed; and as she did so, a trap door beneath her sprang suddenly
open. She dropped, the rush of air blowing up her skirts, revealing
a slogan embroidered in bright blue letters on her pink bloomers.
FORWARD WITH ADULT EDUCATION! they read. (66)

After many more demonstrations of the pointlessness of existence—some exuberantly comic, others meanly depressing—and
after a meaningless sexual encounter, McGoin makes his way
back to his apartment.
     The connection between Eliot and Kees will be explored in
the next chapter, but it is helpful to make some comparisons
here. In *The Waste Land* Eliot closes with some sign of hope.
There is the possibility of putting one's personal life in order,
there is the possibility that some revelation, some drops of in-
vigorating rain, will fall. Kees could never hold out that hope.
The story began with McGoin reading the Bhagavadgita; it ends
with his going back to it:

The Bhagavadgita was even superior to the Koran, which he had
finished the week before. He was nearly through with the Bhagavadgita. Perhaps he could finish it this evening. He was eager to get
on to something else. Listening to the sound of the house across the
street falling in, he decided to start in on Bulfinch's Mythology later
in the week. That was a good one, everyone said. He had heard
nothing but laudatory statements about Bulfinch's Mythology. (72).

Here Kees's vision of the modern world becomes even darker than Eliot's. Eliot believed that the past had value or at least that it had been a far more viable time than the present. Kees is never able to convince himself that the past was any better than the present. And Eliot was sure that there was a spiritual reality somewhere that could redeem man from modern pointlessness. (He eventually found it in Anglo-Catholicism.) Kees had no such assurance, and both points of difference are illustrated here. For these works, dealing with the historical belief-systems of three different cultures, are not prized because they describe mythologies that man once could believe in or because they hold the key to a new syncretic religion. Instead, they are simply a symptom of modern malaise. They hold no real spiritual appeal; they simply constitute interesting reading. They will not save McGoin from anything other than temporary boredom, and they will not save the world.

Speculations

It is interesting to speculate why Kees did not continue to write short fiction in this new vein. In retrospect, he seems to be stopping just when he has been graduated from his apprenticeship. After all, he had finally found a short-story form in which the emphasis was on stylistic effects and narrative technique rather than on magnified character defects. He had also found a world view or at least a way of expressing a world view which came closer to depicting his real dissatisfactions with things as they are more than could any exploration of bourgeois foibles or the effects of economic determinism. In short he could now depict a universe that did not make sense and whose dislocations far outweighed and overshadowed any trivial personal shortcomings. It is as if Kees finally found out what was bothering him—not Mrs. Lutz, but the modern world. And his characters cannot be satirized as those seduced or rendered mindless by the false attractions of this world.

As with so many puzzles, however, the solution to Kees's mysterious abandoning of the short-story form really requires a reorientation of perspective. "The Evening of the Fourth of July" should probably not be seen as the culmination of his career as a short-story writer but instead as a deviation from

his newer career as a poet. For all the techniques employed
in this story—the surreal effects, the expressionistic nightmare
vision, the emphasis on "cultural voices" rather than character—
had already become staples of his poetry. Kees's first poem
was published in 1937. The world of the earlier stories is most
notable for its absence in his poetry. Thus it seems reasonable
to assume that by 1940 Kees felt that his creative urges could
best be expressed in his poetry, even though "The Evening
of the Fourth of July" does demonstrate that he can translate
many of his favorite techniques into highly acceptable short
fiction. Except for one play, Kees's literary creativity, until the
end of his life, would henceforth be channeled into his poetry,
and it is to that, his most significant achievement, we must now
turn.

Chapter Three

The Last Man (1943)

The Last Man, Kees's first volume of verse, was published in San Francisco by the Colt Press as the third in a series of poetry booklets.[1] The poems in the volume reveal that at the same time Kees was writing short stories of social protest and midwestern satire he was composing a very different kind of poetry. Eschewing any commitment to regionalism or economic strife, he sought out the major cosmopolitan poets and movements of his time for inspiration—from T. S. Eliot and W. H. Auden to surrealism and expressionism. (Auden, indeed, was something of a committed left-wing poet in the thirties, and both surrealism and expressionism did have political implications, but these were not the aspects of his models that Kees chose to focus upon.) In essence, he turned to poets and to movements that were avant-garde and appealed to an aesthetic elite.

Such a shift can be applauded simply on the grounds of current aesthetic preference. Auden and Eliot remain major figures today, after all, while most social protest literature has acquired the status of fossils. But in Kees's case there is a far more pertinent reason for valuing the shift. For Kees's poetry gives far greater evidence than his short fiction of the depth of his anguish, the profundity of his pessimism. Life may be stultifying back home on the plains, for example, and economic injustices may abound in the land, but any satire of one or exposé of the other carries with it an implied cure. One can leave the village, after all, and in the future simply associate with those superior individuals who, like the author, are capable of seeing and feeling how folly-ridden life really is. The very concept of temporal injustice suggests a cure is at hand, if only it will be utilized by those sympathetic readers who subscribe to the author's point of view. In short it is a fundamental part of the rhetoric of a fiction like Kees's to appeal to a superior sensibility that is not trapped in the social backwardness or economic misconceptions

that the fiction opposes. And the appeal to that sensibility along
with the smug confidence of the author or narrator is responsible
for the uncomfortable snobbishness that we sometimes noted
in Kees's fiction. In his poetry, Kees was to avoid the snobbish
by taking a far more cosmic view of despair, by insisting that
something far more universal than the dreariness of Depression
life in the Midwest was disturbing him.

Kees, in fact, seldom used local scenes at all in his poetry,
except to make either symbolic or universal points. Notice, for
example, an apparently autobiographical poem, from *The Last
Man,* "For H. V. (1901–1927)":

> I remember the clumsy surgery: the face
> Scarred out of recognition, ruined and not his own.
> Wax hands fattened among pink silk and pinker roses.
> The minister was in fine form that afternoon.
>
> I remember the ferns, the organ faintly out of tune,
> The gray light, the two extended prayers,
> Rain falling on stained glass; the pallbearers,
> Selected by the family, and none of them his friends.

Kees's "I" is certainly not always to be taken autobiographically—it is far more frequently the voice of a detached observer
or poet-figure—but the dates after the subject's name and the
elegiac suggestions of the title and format imply that the poet
is remembering a real person. But in comparison to his short
fiction, there is very little "locating" here in terms of tying
down the poem to one particular section of the country. Morti-
cians' cosmetic skills and perhaps a minister's eloquence are
being quietly satirized, but the sadness of the poet's recollections
does not spring from such foibles or from the mores of one
particular region. Instead, the traditional trappings of grief—
the funeral flowers, the ferns, the gray light—prod the poet's
sad recollection. Even the final obtuseness of the family—their
insensitive selection of pallbearers—is taken as an enhancement
of the grief, not as an occasion for an attack on the dead man's
parents. In short, the tone is radically different from that of
the short stories. The poet is sad because he is in the presence
of the memory of death, whereas the short-story writer would

have been angry because he was in the company of obtuse and unfeeling mourners. Ultimately, the poet is stressing the quality of his recollection of a universally painful event and not stressing the smugness of his superior insight.

Furthermore, when Kees does use a particular setting or geographical area in his poems, he is usually trying to exploit cultural rather than satirical associations. Thus in "Henry James at Newport," one of the more obscure poems of this volume, the only thing that is clear in the poem is Kees's poignant observation of Newport's lifeless present ("The sails are tattered and the shrubs are dead. / The stone-walled fields are featureless."). This inert present is opposed to attitudes stretching from the cosmopolitan, if bloodless, inhabitants of James's days who dreamed of Paris all the way back to the Quakers and Congregationalists of the colonial past. The present vapidity of Newport seems to make the poet discontent, but his discontentment is rooted, somewhat like Eliot's, in a knowledge of past life-styles, not in some quirk of local behavior.

This shift from the smugness of regional satire to the more intractable poignancies of death and historical decay (as well as other themes of universal anguish that we shall see later) had profound implications for Kees's literary career. In the first place, as already noted, Kees becomes a cosmopolitan poet. He now writes about problems that affect the world, from which no man can escape the way a sensitive individual can escape from rural Nebraska to the big city or to the understanding embrace of the literati. He and his readers now enter a new relationship. No longer can they laugh together at the foibles of others: now they must confront their own inescapable destiny, their own share of unsolvable—at least from Kees's point of view—dilemmas. In place of the absurdity of a class or a geographic area, we are now concerned with the absurdity of the world.

Furthermore, because it is the world that is absurd and not just a single individual or group, Kees is able to become part of a tendency that M. A. Rosenthal notes is common among several of the poets of Kees's generation.[2] He can become a confessional poet without becoming intimately autobiographical. That is, he can speak with deep passion and anguish about his doubts concerning the value of existence, without rooting those doubts in personal experiences. The sources of his pessimism, Kees is convinced, lie in the objective universe, not in some hypothetical psychological damage done to him in the past. It is part of Kees's cosmopolitanism, in other words, to assume that he is talking about problems we all face and therefore to see no need to parade idiosyncratic experiences in front of us, or, by and large, to assume that a Freudian psychoanalytical explanation of his or his characters' behavior is in order.

This apparent rejection of psychoanalysis is not simply the rejection of an explanatory mode, however; it is also the rejection of a solution or cure. Kees, as we shall see, knows no cures, rejects all solutions. It is therefore not surprising that Donald Justice can call him "one of the bitterest poets in history."[3] This bitterness or anguish, established primarily before the second world war, was to carry over beyond the war years and make Kees one of the chief examples of postwar, postnuclear-bomb angst.

Because Kees does indulge in so little autobiographical revelation, it is not possible to say exactly why Kees turned from the concerns of his fiction to the concerns of his poetry. But what we shall see in the poems we analyze below is that both aesthetics and world view played a part. That is, he is obviously interested in imitating certain poetic models and he is just as obviously interested in sorting out his own perspective, his own genuine reaction to the world around him. The volume has thirty-nine poems, only three of which run over a page in length. It is divided into three nearly equal parts, and symmetry would seem to be the only justification for the divisions. Thus we will not follow Kees's groupings.

Apprentice Work

Kees found, as the volume shows, the characteristic tone and concerns of his poetry early. He also settled, near the beginning of his career, on those poets who—and aesthetic effects which—would govern his total output. But the first volume understandably includes some efforts more in the nature of student exercises—attempts, irrespective of what would prove to be his natural inclinations, to show that he was indeed a poetic craftsman. These works call attention to themselves as apprentice work rather than as authentic statements of position or inclination.

The most obvious examples in *The Last Man* are "White Collar Ballad," "What the Spider Heard," "A Cornucopia for Daily Use," "Fugue," "Insectae Borinquenses," and "Variations on a Theme by Joyce." They are in no way similar to one another, but they all give evidence of being either heavily derivative or mere exercises in technique of fashion.

"White Collar Ballad," for example, is a rare instance of Kees using a popular form, a self-conscious adaptation of a folk form to the concerns and angst of the bourgeois that had been sanctioned by Auden and others in the 1930s. Although it has a conversational tone and the traditional ballad's incremental refrain (i.e., a line repeated with variations or increments) it really is not a ballad at all. Instead the poem develops as a husband's reflective monologue addressed to his wife. Its subject—here very characteristic of Kees—is the pointlessness of modern life:

> There are lots of places to go:
> Guaranteed headaches at every club,
> Plush and golden cinemas that always show
> How cunningly the heroine and hero rub.
> Put on your hat, put on your gloves.
> But there isn't any love, there isn't any love.

The next two stanzas enumerate the "endless things we could do," but none is very appealing and none will alter the absence of love. The last stanza is more interesting in bringing up one of Kees's more perplexing concerns—that of memory.

> It didn't use to be like this at all.
> You wanted lots of money and I got it somehow.
> Once it was Summer. Here it's almost Fall.
> It isn't any season now.
> There are seasons in the future to be thinking of,
> But there won't be any love, there won't be any love.

Kees's symbolism gets away from him here, probably because in this early work he cannot resolve his own feelings about the importance of one's personal past and memory. The speaker has memories of a past that was different and more valuable.

But now he is caught between seasons—presumably in a time devoid of associations and value, which is certainly the import of the rest of the poem. The problem comes with the prediction that there will be seasons to look forward to in the future. But since there still won't be any love, it is difficult to see just how these new seasons—these periods of meaningful experience—will come about. Symbolism aside, the poem would seem to promise the passage of time but no recurrence of satisfaction or happiness. More to the present point, Kees does not adopt this kind of modern, sophisticated ballad form after this initial effort.

If "White Collar Ballad" may be vaguely or tangentially influenced by Auden, "What the Spider Heard," should be entitled "Variations on Auden," since it is doubtful if it could have been written without a close knowledge of Auden's well-known "The Three Companions." While the content is certainly Kees's own, Auden is the obvious source of the format of brisk questions and answers and the sometimes galloping rhythm.

The parties involved in Kees's drama are a spider, a fly, a chorus, and a stranger who "mysteriously happened by." The spider wishes to know if there will "be time for eggnogs and eclogues / In the place where we're going?" The answer, as the fly, the chorus, and the stranger all make clear, is probably not. Whether this future devoid of libations and poetry is to be the result of the passage of time, an actual physical move, or a switch in intellectual position is deliberately left unclear. What is perfectly clear, however, is that the future is not going to be any better than the past—full of, as the spider is made to realize, beatings, maltreatment, and fear.

Then why go, the spider wants to know. The response shows Kees at his most pessimistic. Disappointment is inevitable, out of control of the rational faculties. All the other speakers make this clear as they jeer at the poor spider:

> What a question! said the fly.
> What a question! sang the chorus.
> What a question! said the stranger,
> Leering slightly at the spider,
> Winking slyly at the fly.

Even more than Auden, T. S. Eliot was a major influence on Kees. But such influence is more assimilated in some works than others. In "A Cornucopia for Daily Use," Kees has pretty much picked up some of Eliot's devices without any attempt to personalize them. The poem begins with the kind of grand, dispassionate tone ("Publish these perils in a colder ice") that Eliot sometimes affects. The work consists, like much in early Eliot, of a series of rapid deflations in tone and shifts in point of view and ostensible subject. It is a collage of clichés.

In dramatic form, with dialogue assigned to a number of speakers, it is also like Eliot's *Waste Land* in containing several passages that do not seem to be assigned to the last identified speaker but to the poet himself. Among the characters are Bones, Sambo, Jessup, Fisher-Barham, Mumford (a dwarf), two strangers, an old man, and someone identified as "A. E. H." The initials must stand for A. E. Housman, the popular late Victorian British poet. At least his one line (delivered "drowsily") sounds like Housman: "Were you a rose-lipped lass when I lifted the sky and shouldered the can?" Mixed in with references to murders and violent ends and fear of death are lines of colloquial speech such as Sambo's "Swell of Lillian to send us these fig newtons," and Jessups's humble, "I always use the three-for-a-dollar kind myself, sir." Needless to say, neither piece of dialogue seems to follow what went before, but the overall effect constitutes a satiric and despairing view of the modern world.

But even some of Eliot's early poems leave little room for hope. With Kees, the ending is different. Cribbing from William Blake, two strangers announce, "We have built Jerusalem in England's green and pleasant land." But the last line belongs to "an old man." "I think I see," he says, "a new process here, a beginning, perhaps; the beginning of the end." In its unfolding, this could be the most masterful line of the poem, since the sentence, right up to its last word, promises optimism, some conventional cause for hope. But all this is taken away by the ultimate noun.

"Fugue" and "Insectae Borinquenses" are perhaps the most self-conscious of all Kees's productions. The former does not closely resemble the contrapuntal pattern of a musical fugue, but there is sufficient repetition of the key terms and rhythms to make the title vaguely appropriate. The title is also appropriate in that it calls attention to the form of the piece rather than to the subject matter, which happens to be the end of the world:

> When the light
> Begins to fail,
> Many now alive
> Will fall.
> Falling night
> Will darken drives,
> Spread the darkness
> Over all.

The short line and the chanting rhythm based on the line's brevity and the irregular alternation of three and four syllables simply make the whole enterprise seem too smug and self-satisfied to be taken seriously. The poem goes on for two more stanzas without changing our judgment, though we do appreciate Kees's poetic dexterity.

"Insectae Borinquenses" is much the same, but the subject matter is sufficiently bizarre or playfully ghoulish as to remove any suspicions that the poet may have serious intentions. The title seems to be Kees's invented Latin name (used in the plural) for a species of insect taking over the earth. The poem achieves its eerie and convincing effect by never allowing itself to become a complete sentence. Instead the movement is through present participles suggestive of the continuing process by which the insects inexorably multiply and spread. The last four lines sum up the nightmare:

> nesting in stumps, attacking caterpillars,
> carrying a legless spider at Coloso—
> thousands upon thousands—
>
> restless forever, and quite indomitable.

Finally, two poems deserve mention because of their attempts to make a connection with the work of earlier masters. "Variations on a Theme by Joyce" has the same kind of verbal repetitions that Kees used in "Fugue" but tied to a simply indecipherable subject. The first line indicates the difficulty: "The war is in words and the wood is the world." The two equations of war and words and wood and world are held together by alliteration and the coordinating conjunction, but their connection is otherwise unapparent and remains so throughout the poem. The remaining lines simply confound the difficulty. The ostensible theme by Joyce is equally obscure.

"On a Painting by Rousseau" is a more successful attempt to capture a painting in verse. The title refers to "Father Juniet's Cart" (1908) by the French primitive Henri Rousseau (1844–1910). The poem's diction is austerely lucid and its tone stately as it describes a family of six sitting in a horse-drawn cart:

> These four and the one in the yellow hat
> Regard us with eyes like photographs
> That have been shown us long ago.
> —All but the man in the driver's seat,
> His wax hands fastened on the reins,
> Who, from the corners of his eyes,
> Watches the horse he does not trust.

Atypical Efforts

In any first volume of poetry, a reader can expect to find a number of efforts that seem inconsistent with the volume as a whole. There are a number of such poems in Kees, some obviously intended to be major efforts. Several of these show a great deal of internal dissension—a sign of a poet trying to come to grips with his self as well as with his technique—others cohere well enough but simply represent roads Kees will not travel in the future.

The second poem of *The Last Man* is a good example of such dissension. Its title, "Statement with Rhymes," sums up neatly what Kees must have thought the purpose of the poem to be. It is both a statement of personal and poetic value. The rhymes are present, but irregular in occurrence. "Plurality is all," Kees begins the poem by stating and repeats at the beginning of the short second stanza. The rest of the first stanza is devoted to a celebration of the varied wonders of the world, the rest of the second to a rejection of the doctrinaire or ideologically rigid mind:

. . . I sympathise, but cannot grieve
too long for those who wear their dialectics on their sleeves.
The pattern's one I sometimes rather like; there's really nothing wrong
with it for some. But I should add: It doesn't wear for long,
before I push the elevator bell and quickly leave.

This rejection of the doctrinaire was never really violated by Kees, which is not surprising since he seldom finds any positive pole or reassuring point of view. In its affirmation of the "plurality" (different cities, gossip, different books and creeds) this poem does strike the positive note that makes it atypical. But that affirmation and exuberance over variety is undercut by some of the details presented. Some of the conversations he overhears on the bus are about "news of the German Jews . . . talk of wars." And no matter what city he is visiting or what technological marvel has propelled him there,

always I'm pursued
by thoughts of what I am, authority,
remembrance, food,
the letter on the mezzanine, the unemployment, dogs' lonely faces,
    pianos and decay

Plurality, then, is a mixed bag. While Kees could try to balance the refreshing and depressing aspects of it for the moment, the latter would soon exert too much weight. Particularly for someone of Kees's sensibility, news of the German Jews would soon sour any talk of "baseball scores."

"Praise to the Mind" is another positive celebration but without an undercurrent of internal conflict. In fact, its relatively serene tone, its gentle and undisturbing imagery combined with its quiet presentation of a placidly self-confident attitude toward reality make it perhaps the most atypical of Kees's poems—a poem no one would think of ascribing to Kees except on the author's word. The line is again short, running from four to six syllables, and each of the three six-line stanzas offers a variation on the kind of mind Kees wants to praise. The first stanza celebrates the mind "That slowly grows / In solid breadth" and will admit its own limitations. The second stanza offers the most complex aspect to be praised:

        Praise to the single mind
        That sees no street
        Run through this world, complete,
        That does not meet,
        Bending at end,
        Remorselessly, its source.

Such an integrated vision was never to be Kees's nor, apparently, was ever to be praised after this early effort.

Two other poems, "The Caterpillar and the Men from Cambridge" and "Obituary" show Kees trying, in a manner Auden had made respectable, to be the occasional poet. One writes an occasional poem not out of the inexorable impulses of the psyche or because he is driven by a vision of organic wholeness but in response to a local happening, to celebrate a passing event, or just to note a momentary reflection.

"Caterpillar" is occasioned by a passage in Ogden and Richard's *The Meaning of Meaning* that describes the way a chicken becomes conditioned to avoid foul-tasting caterpillars. Kees thinks the experiment is interesting but faults Ogden and Richards for leaving out those elements which make the experiment a good "story." What happened to the chicken, to the observing scientist? And what about the poor worm? "Did it suffer? Is anything heard / Of this martyr to science, this pitiful bait?"

"Obituary" does not celebrate a martyr to science but the passing of an anarchist parrot, Boris, who used to cry, "Out, brief candle," and "Down with tyranny, hate, and war!" The poem is a beautiful rendering of grief in the best modern way, stately and without any untoward personal emotion. In fact, it is almost as reserved as John Crowe Ransom's stony "Bells for John Whiteside's Daughter." But, despite the gloomy subject matter, Kees draws no general conclusions. It is a single death and not the condition of the world he is lamenting.

The most impressive and complex of all these atypical efforts is "After the Trial." Kees obviously has a Kafkaesque trial in mind, and the poem is unique in Kees's canon for refocusing the source of angst from the condition of the world to the more Freudian condition of the family and the more specific relationship between parents and child.

The poem begins with a third-person description of the "prisoner's feeling" on "hearing the judges' well-considered sentence" and the unusual presence of more than one judge tends to suggest the nightmarish quality the poem will evoke. The prisoner, though innocent, is obviously a haunted man:

> The prisoner saw long plateaus of guilt,
> And thought of all the dismal furnished rooms

The past assembled, the eyes of parents
Staring through walls as though forever
To condemn and wound his innocence.

The use of the objective third-person allows us to see that the prisoner is indeed innocent, though hardly at ease. The paranoia of his parents, staring through the dismal walls of the past, manages to make him extremely unpleasant. The second stanza shifts to the first person and the prisoner describes his own dilemma. He realizes that he could stand screaming forever and not manage to erase the judges' verdict. In an arresting public metaphor for a private (familial) force he concludes that "All the machinery of law devised by parents / Could not be stopped though fire swept the rooms." Note that it is not *my* parents but simply "parents." This holds true for every occurrence of "parents" in the poem. Obviously it is the presence of parents in the world and the relationship between child and parents that lies at the center of the poem— not one particular relationship. In the speaker's case, convinced that he can never escape the guilt parents have laid on him, he looks forward to death, to being "escorted to the silent rooms / Where darkness promises a final sentence." Despite the escort, the ultimate means of destruction here is suicide—the destruction of a self unable to rid itself of guilt.

In the final three lines of the poem, the voice again shifts to first person plural, as the poet draws the final, generalizing conclusion.

We walk forever to the doors of guilt,
Pursued by our own sentences and eyes of parents,
Never to enter innocent and quiet rooms.

This conclusion performs the rhetorical function of underscoring the poet's intention of including all of us throughout. As noted, it is interesting that an individual as racked by guilt and angst as Kees must have been did not return to this essentially psychological or psychoanalytical exploration of the human condition. But the reason he did not is apparent in "After the Trial" itself. Even here, Kees is not exploring just his own past, but the past of all. He is convinced that whatever the problem is, it

lies with the world, not just him. Rather than probing one neurotic individual, the body of his poetry is primarily devoted
to exploring that more objective dilemma.

A Matter of Perspective

While Kees's attitude is apparent throughout the volume,
several poems are more directly committed to stating that perspective rather than simply leaving the reader to infer it. For
example, "For My Daughter," perhaps the most bitter poem
in the collection, is a direct statement of Kees's view of the
horror of modern life. As the speaker looks deeply into his
daughter's eyes, he sees all the misfortune the young child can
have in store for her. It is symptomatic of Kees's thinking that
the misfortunes—all repellent—are a mixed bag. That is, some
are very much a product of the modern moment, others are
perennial afflictions of mankind. Thus death, old age, and "the
night's slow poison" certainly await her but only if she is lucky
enough to escape "a foul lingering / Death in certain war,
the slim legs green." Even if she could avoid death in a war,
her mind may become twisted and monstrous in the climate
of the times until "fed on hate, she relishes the sting / Of
others' agony." But it is the shocking last line that indelibly
sets out the extremity of Kees's bitterness. The poet has been
deceiving his readers, misrepresenting his parenthood: "I have
no daughter. I desire none."

In "The Speakers" Kees makes even clearer why he never
would have desired a daughter and publicly announces his dis-
agreement on one particular point with Eliot. The first stanza
of the poem is a slightly sardonic rendering of modern befud-
dlement. Three speakers cannot agree whether "A equals X"
or "B" or "nothing under the sun / But A." Some hearing
the debate are amused, some are sad, and some linger to
watch two of the debaters "in neat disguise / Decapitating" the
third.

The second and last stanza, however, shows the poet in his
own voice undercutting any attempt at nostalgia for a past unlike
the present. The present age is bad enough, the poet admits,
but the reader

Should know Elizabethans had
Sweeneys and Mrs. Porters too.
The past goes down and disappears,
The present stumbles home to bed,
That future stretches out in years
That no one knows, and you'll be dead.

Sweeney and Mrs. Porter are recurrent characters in Eliot's
poems. Apeneck Sweeney represents sexual energy and impulse
cut off from any rational control. Mrs. Porter represents the
depravity and degeneration of modern feminine sexuality. She
is usually a brothel-keeper, and there is more than a suggestion
that some of the prostitutes working for her are actually her
daughters. Kees does not deny the characters' repulsiveness,
simply their uniqueness to the present. Conversely, Eliot often
used the Elizabethan period as a point of ironic contrast to the
modern. In insisting on the two periods' essential sameness,
Kees is insisting that we cannot find value—as Eliot tries to—
by returning to the past. Eliot's famous return to the Anglican
church that Elizabeth's father Henry VIII started, along with
his return to classicism in literature and to royalism in politics,
was an insistence on the value of returning to one's roots. By
imitating the past, by eschewing modern "heresies," a mind
could find solace and integration. Perhaps Eliot did indeed find
these qualities, but Kees sees well enough that no such road
is available to him. He could not develop a dialectic like Eliot's
that counterpoised past and present and implied that salvation
will lie either in our swinging back to the past or in generating
a new synthesis out of the two extremes. Instead Kees is faced
with a linear continuum. At one extreme the past dips below
the horizon; at the other, the future is indecipherable. It is a
pointless vista that in any case will be canceled out by the death
of the individual. Eliot would remain a poetic influence, but
his search for personal value obviously held little for Kees.

   Though Eliot is not mentioned explicitly in "To the North,"
Kees has in mind those like Eliot who can find redemption in
the past. The "North" of the title is symbolic of our modern
cold and comfortless desolation, where man is reduced to "burrowing" to stay warm. Others in their burrowing can "find
some acre of the past to praise." Kees cannot and instead is
confronted with the "countertruth" he has already expressed

less forcefully in "The Speakers." The past consists of "the days / Of other whippings, exiles, sicknesses," and the "horror of history."

If time or history offers no hope, it is effectively dead. But "Where is [its] grave? . . ." Since time is meaningless in any ideational sense, since it carries no purposiveness that can appeal to the intellect, Kees is reduced to rendering the grave imagistically:

> . . . What would you picture for decay?
> A horse's hoof, white bones, a lifeless tree,
> Cold hemispheres, dried moss, and a blue wave
> Breaking at noon on shores you will not see.

All that remains are the aesthetically pleasing but spiritually useless reminders that life has gone on before and an image of a future without us.

The last image of a wave breaking against the shore at noon is perhaps the master stroke of the poem. It is not as cold or marmoreal as the other lifeless items; in fact, it teems with activity and presumably the warmth of the noonday sun. Indeed it is really not an image of decay. But it takes place after our decay or death and is therefore bereft of meaning for anyone without a sense of Christian immortality or pantheistic survival. In the whole last passage, but especially here, Kees is able to offer the aesthetically beautiful and to indicate simultaneously the inadequacy of aesthetics to deal with certain human dilemmas.

"When the Lease is Up" is certainly a lesser effort, but still enunciates Kees's insistence that the world is a botched affair. This time, however, he is only concerned with the present. The poem is written in the second person, but the "you" being addressed is decidedly impersonal—and universal. The poem ignores the cause for the distress, in order to concentrate on instructions for what to do, now that *"the lease is up, the time is near."* Kees turns the ordinary into the macabre by the addition of a few details: the horses have to be walked "through the *darkening* groves"; even the "eyeless cat" senses things are going bad; and, in our paranoia, we must "darken the rooms" and "cut all the wires." Perhaps one can survive the times if he can simply hide out.

"To a Contemporary" is also written in the second person.
Kees may have had a particular individual in mind, but the
poem functions as a rejection of the type of cold, cruel aesthete
who savors his aesthetic and sexual experiences more than the
companionship of other humans. The poem is prefaced with a
quotation from Baudelaire, which translates into "I have more
memories than if I had lived a thousand years." Perhaps this
was true for Baudelaire, but Kees obviously finds it less so for
our dilettante. "Memories rich as Proust's and Baudelaire's are
yours / You think," Kees taunts him at the beginning of the
poem and then begins to enumerate the memories. Bodies of
women, arguments "with undistinguished friends," unfamiliar
lamplit faces in cafes, and strange boudoirs. The dilettante frequently compares himself to others whose recollections "are
cruel, contemptible, like naked bone." Again, the stark aesthetic
image of naked bone has its appeal, but for Kees it does not
connote a satisfactory life:

> Yet, is there anything in this rank richness warm
> Or permanent? At every climax, trapped, alone,
> You seem to be a helpless passenger that drifts
> On some frail boat; and with oblivious ease,
> As from a distance, watch yourself
> Disintegrate in foaming seas.

Perhaps Kees's most effective and obvious attempt to speak
his mind on a public issue is "June 1940." It is in some ways
reminiscent of Auden's famous "September 1939," another
poem lamenting the onset of World War II. Auden's, however,
takes place in public, in a bar on 42nd street; Kees's, characteris-
tically, is set in a darkened room where the speaker is alone
at midnight. Kees prefaces the poem with two quotations from
the most famous antiwar poet of the earlier war, Wilfred Owen.
The first is from Owen's preface to his posthumously published
poems:

Yet these elegies are to this generation in no sense consolatory. They
may be to the next. All a poet can do today is warn.

The second is from perhaps his best known war poem: "The
Old Lie: Dulce et decorum est pro patria mori." The first four

words of the Latin are the poem's title and the whole phrase means "Sweet and fitting it is to die for one's country." The quotation aptly expresses Kees's bitterness at seeing another war on the horizon and associates him with Owen in the latter's hatred of all the hypocrisies of war and patriotism. The first quotation, however, is more Eliotic in function, since the advent of another war makes clear that Owen's warnings were for naught. Kees will not try to warn but simply express his own sense of frustration.

The epigraphs having established the general attitude, Kees begins the poem by establishing the setting for his current thoughts. This strategy of making the thought rise out of a particular setting has the effect of making one's observations more cogent and psychologically valid since the reader can perceive the actual environment—both mental and physical—out of which the poet's reflections arise:

> It is summer, and treachery blurs with the sounds of midnight,
> The lights blink off at the closing of a door,
> And I am alone in a worn-out town in wartime,
> Thinking of those who were trapped by hysteria once before.

The first line is very long (fifteen syllables), and its two independent clauses and long arhythmic consonantal sound tend to make it even more somber and more deliberative. The tone also makes it clear that the hysteria in the last line is not a phenomenon spawned by the poet's mind. Indeed, it is the warmonger's hysteria which has trapped so many innocents in its fury.

In the second stanza the speaker recalls other writers from the past who have been damaged by such hysteria, from Flaubert and Owen to Rilke, Lawrence, and Joyce. All, according to Kees, hated war, were "gun-shy," but all "Suffered the same attack till it broke them or left its scars."

The third stanza is perhaps the most bitter, "now the heroes of March are the sorriest fools of April. . . ." These heroes are the pacifists who were once against war, once spurred on the conscience to reject all wars. Now they have changed, have become "the beaters of drums, the flag-kissing men." Where they once recognized war for the murder Kees thinks it is, now they only accuse their fellow believers: "You are the cowards! All that we told you before was lies!"

But now it is neither March nor April, but summer. And Kees once again reminds the reader that the "windows are dark" and "the mountains are miles away." The last detail is a beautiful example of how the prosaic can soar into symbolism in the right context. Why the detail is there we cannot know for sure, but we sense that it is not purely geographical. Surely the poet is saying that any thought of refuge, any thought of hiding out during the coming storm is simply impossible. Meanwhile, continuing his bitterness to the end, he notes that the "heroes" of the third stanza are active again, mounting their speakers' platforms. With the sound of their voices, "An idiot wind is blowing; the conscience dies." Kees cannot summon up a visionary maelstrom like Yeats in "Meditations in Time of Civil War" or "Nineteen Hundred and Nineteen" to describe this death of conscience and the onset of the symbolic wind, but then his tone suggests he does not share Yeats's hope that something worthwhile lies beyond such difficulties. The tone remains true to the end. It is one of quiet despair, devoid of the hope that something could be done to change things.

Of course, nothing was done, and it is worth noting that whatever Kees's ultimate thoughts about the war might have been, he never wrote the kind of war poetry associated with some of his contemporaries like Randal Jarrell. Kees lacked Jarrell's first-hand experience of the war, but, equally significant, his general morbid view of reality prevented him from seeing the war as an aberration or as an extraordinarily cataclysmic event.

The Surreal and the Expressionistic

As everyone who has studied T. S. Eliot's "Love Song of J. Alfred Prufrock" knows, when the evening is described as being "spread out against the sky / like a patient etherized upon a table," the image invoked is expressionistic. That is, the description is a figment of the mind of the character, J. Alfred Prufrock, not an attempt at a mimetic representation of nature. Similiarly, when we meet a sentence like "Eagles with tusks perform in sieves," we are apt to describe both the image and the action depicted as surreal. And "surreal" can also be defined as something beyond (or above or below) realism or of mimetic repre-

sentation. Expressionism, as a movement in art, had its origins
in Germany immediately before the first world war, surrealism
in France between the wars. And while it is very easy, in painting,
to separate the German from the French, it is much harder in
literature, especially in American literature where both terms
have become generalized and vague and where neither school
has had major representation. Thus it is very easy to say that
throughout his poetry Kees often chose the nonrepresentational
image; it is much harder to decide whether his imagery is decidedly surreal or expressionistic. Perhaps either term is fashionable
enough to do the job. But we can make distinctions in Kees's
use of such imagery based on some of the differences in world
view that separated expressionism, as a movement, from surrealism.

The example of a surreal line given above occurs in Kees's
poem, "Corsage." The poem abounds with such imagery—in
fact, it is a poem about "mind's residue," the various and slightly
incoherent leavings of a mind in revery. In the first stanza,
Kees, probably with surrealistic painting in mind, describes the
mind's hoard in terms of colors. It is "vein-violet (old women
with their stockings hanging down)—gorged with color and
superb as light." The second stanza is devoted to reveries or
daydreams which occur while the speaker claims to be in an
empty park. Sometimes he hears

> the rustle of revival-meeting
> pamphlets. Band music, with
> surrealistic trumpets, knifes the air.
> Eagles with tusks perform in sieves.
> The ectoplasm of Immanuel Kant unwittingly
> appears.

In the last lines of this poem Kees describes the images above
as being "profound, perfect, and / not without meaning." That
meaning is never given, and most doctrinaire surrealists would
insist that such a meaning could not be rendered in rational,
logical terms in any case, since the whole purpose of surrealistic
technique is to free the psyche from the constraints of the natural
world. Once such liberation occurred, revolution of a more
or less Dionysian variety would surely follow. Kees never had

much faith in Dionysian revolution, but in the passage described above he does seem to be taking a great interest in the sheer joy of the images. None of them is threatening or nightmarish in any horrific sense, and even the unwilling appearance of Immanuel Kant ("ectoplasm" is a term in spiritualism describing the part of a being actually recalled by the medium during a seance) is actually a mild sophomoric joke aimed at the philosopher who insists we could not prove the existence of the noumenal (i.e., nonempirical) world.

The expressionists had revolutionary pretensions, too, but their imagery was not designed to liberate the psyche. It was designed to reveal the mindless enslavement of modern man. The term "nightmare," therefore, is far more appropriate to expressionism. Prufrock's image of the evening reveals a mind that sees itself trapped by society and convention, but Eliot tends to blame Prufrock as much as he does "polite" society. The German expressionists were far more explicit in making man the pawn and civilization or the state the oppressor. Kees tends not to isolate the oppressor; for him we are simply caught in bad times, and his nonrepresentational imagery is designed to bring out the fact.

If the title "Corsage" suggests that all the associations in the poem combine to make something as attractive as a flower, the titles of three other poems redolent with expressionistic imagery—"The Inquiry," "Scream as You Leave," and "Stale Weather"—suggest the fear, ugliness, and angst of modern life.

"The Inquiry," for example, has none of the playfulness of "Corsage." It is set in dialogue form, but, despite the title, it is not a judicial inquiry. There are no adversaries; questioner and answerers are in total agreement, and the poem is full of horrific images such as the "keyhole's splintered eye," which, in proper paranoidal fashion, is feared. And the last lines of the poem are the questioner's prediction that the other voice will soon have more to fear, will soon have to walk barefoot and blindfolded through streets "full of broken glass." All of this is relayed with an absolutely somber tone which reinforces both the deterministic, trapped world of the expressionists and the nightmarish quality of their vision.

"Scream as You Leave," on the other hand, could just as easily be considered as playful as "Corsage" if it were not for hints of Kees's attitude here and there and the perfectly ominous title. After all, couplets like "Impromptu unicorns enact ballets / Applauded by bourgeoisie in negligee," have as much of the comic in them as they do of the satiric, and the whole image is far too bouyant to be totally despairing. Nevertheless, Kees cannot enjoy these creations of his unfettered imagination for very long, and he is soon proclaiming the end of the world: "The weather wrinkles to a shrunken end." "Stale Weather" strikes more of a compromise. It intermixes its balladlike refrain (*"The rusty bird sang a song about graves"*) with images both unbridled and pessimistic:

> A dead fish floats voluptuously
> Across the landscape, clear and blue;
> Its neon mouth flashes, "Vote for McGee,"
> While over its head is a halo or two.

After three stanzas full of death and oppression—but also full of exuberant imagery of fishes with neon mouths and "reversible horses leak[ing] gallons of ale"—the last stanza becomes more somber, and "Out of a cloud comes a hollow wail, / And a purple stain spreads over the skies." But even here the stain is purple, not blood red.

Obviously, we must conclude that Kees draws on both traditions as sources or models for his nonrepresentational imagery. Hereafter, when it is worthy of note, we will use the terms "expressionistic" or "surrealistic" to describe the imagery consistent with the definitions given above. But such nonrepresentational imagery in Kees is so pervasive, that it will doubtless often be cited without any term attached, especially when it is used to reinforce a thematic point.

The Social Tone

T. S. Eliot's early verse often managed to be socially satiric—that is, it often made fun of the pretensions of society by mocking its affectations. For example, the very name, J. Alfred Prufrock, is in part designed to type the character as a rather stuffy member of a certain strata of society. Some of the dialogue in the *Waste Land,* such as its mocking of high society's acceptance of ragtime

("O O O O that Shakespeherian Rag") has similar designs.
Despite his dislike of the modern world, Kees shared Eliot's
talent and a desire to exploit the foibles of high—and sometimes
low—society. In a poem like "The Situation Clarified," for example, the debt to Eliot is obvious. A crime—possibly murder,
possibly something more sexually scandalous—has been committed, and the victim resembles Eliot's Prufrock in a number of
ways. He is a "frightened male librarian," slightly past his youth
and showing signs of baldness. His end is apparently a little
more gruesome than Prufrock's fantasy retreat among the mer-
maids but just as hard to imagine. After gyrating "most consider-
ately / Through all the latest books," he is hung by wires from
rafters by a strangely bitter and bewigged denizen named Jones.
(" 'Jones is my name,' he said.")
    Whatever the scandalous circumstances, the crime is hushed
up more or less immediately by an "anonymous friend / Of
the Carnegie family." And so, the speaker concludes in the
most bitter moment of the poem, "Justice triumphed in the
end." But unfortunately the end didn't come in time to keep
"dear Mrs. Cudlip-Finch" from a recurrence of her old pains
in the duodenum. The delight in this piece of "inside" information and the satiric potential of the hyphenated proper name
(worthy of Eliot in its incongruity) keep the bitterness at bay,
of course, and show Kees to be capable of a great deal of urbanity. Given Kees's generally dour outlook, this urbanity may
be surprising, but it was a tone and an attitude that Kees was
to use many times throughout his career.
    In its own way, it becomes something of a talisman or earnest
of his situation. His attack on the values of civilization, in other
words, is not based on social exclusion or his inability to conform
at a strictly social level.
    In fact, when Kees does write about the manners of the
wealthy or the socially comfortable, just about the only thing
that makes him lose the urbane tone is boredom. In "Resort,"
for example, his somber and detached tone never really achieves
the kind of urbane satirical surface of "The Situation Clarified."
The poem celebrates the closing of a vacation boarding house,
but all of the memories of the past summer simply seem to
reinforce the ennui of life.

The clerk that opened everybody's mail;
The woman who put sugar in her beer;
One frame-up, one divorce, one minor theft.
"Goodbye, goodbye! We shall be back again next year!"

One gets some sense of the absurdity of life from the juxtaposi-tion of the mindless last line with the series of unappealing collections that have preceded it, but none of the memories simply lend themselves to treatment as the foibles of a particular class or as signs of an especially foolish or degenerate society.

But when Kees wishes to combine the urbane with the hor-rific, he is much more successful. "The Party" is really a predic-tion of the carnage and destruction of the coming war. It gets most of its power from being set at a mindless cocktail party presided over by an "obscene hostess" and an "unconvincing oriental" whom she has called on to produce a vision in a crystal ball. Mrs. Lefevre "with her one good eye" is one of the guests, and as they gather around the ball, "A friendly abdomen rubs against one's back; / 'Interesting,' a portly man is heard to sigh." As sulfurous smoke emanates from the globe and the party's guests become even more excited, a scene suddenly invades the glass, bringing silence to the room:

Our eyes
Stare at the planes that fill the swelling globe,
Smoke-blue; blood, shell-torn faces. Suddenly a drum
Begins its steady beat, pursues us even here;
Death, and death again, and all the wars to come.

The juxtaposition of a somewhat "wicked" cocktail party of the 1920s or 1930s with the absolute horror of warfare seems to work perfectly here, with social satire of the first lines making its point and then reinforcing and interfering with the extremely frightening effect of the latter.

Much the same effect, although even more macabre, is ob-tained in "The View of the Castle," where a fairly cultivated speaker is explaining to his wife the demise of the dwelling's royal family. Kees achieves much of his effect by juxtaposing modern idiom with an account of a medieval castle and a presum-ably long extinct royal line, reminiscent of Eliot's collapsing

of time. "The castle is mortgaged now, my dear," the monologue begins, and for the next two stanzas goes on to describe
the fallen and decayed state of the edifice. Of course, one has
to assume some symbolic value, but Kees is careful not to introduce any specific referent. In the third stanza, we get more
shocking news. "The princesses were whores, my dear," and
neither king nor queen is really much surprised at this or that
the prince apparently had venereal disease. So much for the
decayed castle and the doomed family. In the last stanza the
speaker promises to show his wife other historic sights of almost
equal value: "Battlegrounds, parks . . . hundreds of monuments
to war." Thus the poem is about the folly of man and at the
same time demonstrates Kees's unwillingness to accept any redemption or comfort from the past. But in this poem, with its
repetition of "my dear" scattered throughout, the speaker keeps
his informative and colloquial demeanor as he retells the trag-
edy.

Narratives and Antinarratives

Kees does not attempt any long narrative poem in his first
volume. But there are occasions where he takes advantage of
anecdotal material or draws upon the conventional expectations
or forms of narrative to make what is essentially a reflective
point. In "Aunt Elizabeth," for example, it is obvious that Kees
is more interested in exploring the mind of an old, "respectable"
woman, bereft of everything but that respectability, than he is
in really developing an action. Aunt Elizabeth herself, as the
dramatized narrator, Paul, tells us more than once, is imprisoned
by the past. The first line of the poem describes the pictures
of her proper ancestors ("hideous" according to the narrator)
looking down on her. Aunt Elizabeth sits under them, not only
imprisoned by them but also by old plants and the chair she
is sitting in, which her mother died in. But in perhaps the best
insight of the poem, Kees has her imprisoned not only by her
past and her current surroundings but has her memory "rear-
ranged by hardening arteries" and that part of the past she
chooses to—and her arteries allow her to—recall.

But this is hardly even anecdotal. Kees makes this a narrative
by having her recount the one horror in her life—mysterious

phone calls which, when answered, turn out to be dead lines. The dead lines could represent the essential lack of vital connection with the past or her lack of connection with present-day reality. In any event, the narrator reaches for an even more macabre effect. After describing Aunt Elizabeth's window as a "glass[ing] out" of the afternoon—a great image of her isolation—he gives us the shocker: "And there has been no telephone for years."

On the same subject of elderly relatives, "Lines for an Album" is even less of a narrative. In fact, the only narrative element is a borrowed refrain ("Over the river and through the woods / To Grandmother's house we go") inserted at the beginning and end of the poem. What (or whom) the grandchildren find on arrival is the subject of the body of the poem. In his description of the grandmother, Kees is interested in drawing out the horrific. The contrast between the gaiety of the refrain and the broken woman waiting at the end of the journey is too extreme for there to be any genuine shock. We feel, in other words, that the poet has designs upon us. But there are some fine images in the picture of the old woman "with her toothless smile and enuresis [involuntary urination]."

If "Lines for an Album" plays on the notion of the distance between reality and the popular expectations of a mindless song, "The Forests" exploits our sense of conventional ending. The poem describes the struggle to escape of a man lost in the forest and his eventual, hard-won exultant success. But the exultation is short lived, for the man is in a symbolic landscape where allegorical forests are an everyday occurrence. Thus he soon "thought of the other forests beyond."

Perhaps in a slightly more complex way, "The Scene of the Crime" plays on our moral expectations as well as our narrative ones. "There should have been some witness there, accusing," the poem begins. But there is no witness, the crime takes place in obscure circumstances, and even the moral outrage of the speaker—"there should have been damnation"—is met with silence. We are simply left with a meaningless murder that neither art nor morality can make sense of. Kees probably uses too weak a vehicle for an attack on the valuelessness or meaninglessness of the universe.

A Question of Style

Now that we have seen a wide range of Kees's work, we are in a position to make some general observations about his style. Donald Justice, perhaps unwittingly, strikes the central note of paradox that must govern any such discussion:

> To originality in style and technique his poetry would seem to lay little claim. Yet since the whole style of his poetry lies in its very unobtrusiveness, it is a crucial part of his individual tone. It is a style which answers to what seems to me the classical definition of a good *prose* style: natural words in a natural order. His work, in fact, belongs to what might be called the Prose Tradition in poetry.
>
> This is not to say that Kees ignores the technical matters which are the major concerns of another type of poet. Many of his forms are formal. He toys with the villanelle and that elaborate form the sestina.[4]

We shall see more self-conscious use of such formal types in his subsequent volumes, but obviously it is very difficult to see how a poet can be both "natural" and intrigued by poetic artifice. Furthermore, there is nothing wrong with being a "prose" poet—many of Kees's contemporaries and models write poetry which does not violate normal English syntax.

But perhaps our sense of Kees as a poet who is not always prosaic does not rest in his use of syntax. There are, after all, other ways to violate the normal expectations of good prose. One is to disturb the reader through the lexis or diction. To use a term coined by modern linguistics, Kees often, especially in his surreal and expressionistic works, indulges in collocational shifts. That is, he disturbs our sense of the normal distribution of English diction. When, for example, he writes, in a passage we have already seen from "Stale Weather":

> A dead fish floats voluptuously
> Across the landscape, clear and blue;
> Its neon mouth flashes, "Vote for McGee,"
> While over its head is a halo or two.

we do not feel that we are in the environs of standard English prose. But it is not the syntax that disturbs our sense of the normal; rather, it is the unexpected appearance of certain lexical items. We do not expect "voluptuously" to describe a floating dead fish, do not expect a landscape to be "blue," do not expect a fish to have a "neon" mouth or a "halo or two" over its head. Thus any account of Kees's "prosiness" is going to have to distinguish sharply, as Justice does not, between his syntax and his lexical choices.

And, obviously, the effect of these lexical choices, these violations of normal collocational ranges, is to make the reader aware that he is in the presence of the poetic, of a consciously rendered artifact which must be examined for something other than the bare "information" it conveys.

But at the level of syntax, Justice is certainly right. In general we can agree that, like good prose, Kees's poetry seldom calls attention to itself by violating ordinary English syntax, by offering sentence patterns which seem "ungrammatical" to a native speaker, by indulging in obviously overwrought rhetorical patterns alien to modern sensibility, or by imposing a highly noticeable and artificial rhythm on itself. It is these restraints, doubtless, which give Kees the cool, understated and unemotional tone which he so often seeks.

But even in the most "prosiac" of his poems, other stylistic features are at work, features which force us to respond to the work in question as "poetic." At its most basic level, Kees's work is poetic because it observes certain typographic conventions that make the individual line a potential unit of meaning—something that never occurs with prose. Furthermore, Kees indulges in all sorts of other poetic conventions. He uses rhyme and half-rhyme on occasion. His metaphoric density works against the swift access to meaning that we expect from ordinary prose. His imagery often functions in a similar fashion, being less than immediately apprehensible in the interest of a more powerful and delayed effect. And meaning is often further postponed by the lack of obvious connections or transitions, and by a propensity for the aphoristic or oracular statement which must be interpreted without recourse to mundane explanations or elaborations on the part of the poet. In short, Kees's various stylistic tactics often demand the kind of behavior on the part of the reader that we associate with poetry, not prose.

We must, therefore, expand Justice's paradoxical opposition

of prose and an interest in formal verse patterns to include various other techniques and strategies which cut against the expectations of prose. Syntactically and often tonally, then, Kees's style may be indistinguishable from that of good prose, but it also contains a number of other features which guarantee its essential poeticalness.

Conclusion

All in all, *The Last Man* is a remarkable first volume. Especially when considered against the bulk of his fiction, it shows a remarkable broadening of technical awareness and resources, and a much more comprehensive and resonant world view. Much, perhaps, is too derivative; but that is likely to be any young poet's failing. What is more noteworthy are the signs that a unique poetic voice is being born, a voice that can retain its uniqueness while borrowing from the best poets of the generation before him. Certainly any reader of poetry in the 1940s coming across this volume would have every reason to look forward to the poet's subsequent efforts.

Chapter Four

The Fall of Magicians (1947)

Unlike the publishers of Kees's first volume, Reynall and Hitchchock, publisher of the second, was a newly organized and ambitious New York trade house, determined to develop a quality list. Among its other notable publications was an illustrated edition of Coleridge's *Rime of the Ancient Mariner,* with a long commentary by Robert Penn Warren. Warren's commentary is remembered even today as one of the first and most controversial studies in New Criticism. Their publishing of Kees certainly says something about the way he had managed to establish a reputation for himself in influential circles.

In fact, the evidence suggests that Kees was not quite ready to publish another volume. Like the first volume, *The Fall of Magicians* is subdivided into numbered units—units which seem to serve typographical convenience since there is no overriding thematic or formal justification for them. But the fourth and last unit is made up of thirteen poems previously published in *The Last Man.* Kees chose to reprint the following: "Variations on a Theme by Joyce," "Praise to the Mind," "White Collar Ballad," "For My Daughter," "For H. V. (1901–1927)," "After the Trial," "A Cornucopia for Daily Use," "Aunt Elizabeth," "Early Winter," "To The North," "Obituary," "The View of the Castle," "The Smiles of the Bathers." Needless to say, his choices—some of which we have analyzed—are baffling. Apprentice work rubs shoulders with solid efforts. Perhaps the selection simply proves that Kees, like many writers, was not a particularly good critic of his own work. Whatever the cause, Donald Justice wisely reprinted the thirteen in the *Collected Poems* where they rightly belong, as part of *The Last Man,* and we will not include them in our discussion of *The Fall of Magicians.* [1]

Thus we are left with a rather slender selection of new poems, twenty-six in all. But among those twenty-six are some genuinely fine efforts. We will, of course, see Kees continuing in a number of different poems to brood on the significance of the past and human memory. Such brooding, in fact, will be the occasion for his most ambitious poem to date, "Eight Variations," in which he explores various ramifications of the past through a series of fourteen-line meditations. We will also see him find new targets for his satiric sensibility, as well as revisit some old ones. And this volume will mark the peak of his interest in formal verse patterns, patterns in which the poet is challenged to be both meaningful and lucid within a precisely defined and highly artificial format.

Finally, we will examine a set of poems which could be grouped in any number of ways, but which we have chosen to examine in terms of Kees's varying degrees of poetic sincerity. Kees, in other words, could adopt the stance of the purely lyric poet, speaking from his poet's heart without any attempt at adopting the voice or mask of a dramatic or "other" character; he could just as easily speak through a voice clearly meant to be identified with someone other than the poet. The permutations within these two extremes give a good indication of the range of Kees's point of view and show that, despite his highly pessimistic view of things, he did not for a minute feel it necessary to lock himself in the prison of his own mind.

Prurient Tapirs and Asthmatic Bulldogs

The first poem of Kees's second volume indicates that he is trying to extend his range and his virtuosity. Entitled "Eight Variations," it is an assembly of eight fourteen-line poems (not sonnets—they lack the conventional or even a common stanza division and alternate between poems of ten-syllable lines and twelve). Only one of the poems is individually titled, and that title does not go far in answering the obvious question: variations on what? Perhaps the reference is to the variations on the fourteen-line model; but I suspect that Kees's real variation is thematic, for all these poems deal with the value, or lack thereof, of the past. Far more systematically than in the first volume, Kees attempts to remove any solace from the past, to exorcise it of any lingering and meaningful nostalgia, and to reject certain life-styles which are rooted in the past. Only in the last poem does he manage to see any redemptive value in the recall of past times.

The first poem in the series has three four-line stanzas followed by two concluding lines spaced as if separate stanzas. The stanzas are all based on an opposition between past and present, introducing various personal memories which somehow do not help the fallen present, despite their attractiveness. The first stanza, however, would lead one to assume that the whole poem is to be about erotic experience:

> Prurient tapirs gamboled on our lawns,
> But that was quite some time ago.
> Now one is accosted by asthmatic bulldogs,
> Sluggish in the hedges, ruminant.[2]

One can see that Kees's penchant for surreal images has not left him, though it is still difficult to appreciate prurience in the piglike tapir. Yet the essential contrast is clear enough. The erotic gamboling of the past has been replaced by bovine wheezing, and the poem goes on to suggest further problems. In the second stanza the scene shifts from the lawn to a park, but time has wrought similar changes. The waterfalls are "drying," the "grave, shell-white unicorn is gone," and only litter remains. Apparently, a more abstract, aesthetic sense of beauty has left the lovers' world as well. Stanza three is less satisfactory because Kees seems to be dealing with an abstraction ("numbers") as if it had some tangible sense. Thus the lovers were once "regarded" by numbers so significant as to attract the attention of the press. But now all is a monotone as the tired "bell strikes one, strikes one. . . ."

If this poem is a recollection of a pleasant past which has not survived into the present, the second poem is an obvious attempt at exorcising an unpleasant past whose memories still bedevil the present. It is the only one with a title: "Note to Be Left on the Table." A speaker of uncertain gender attempts to vanquish the memory of a dead male lover/friend. Most of the power comes from the strong exaggerated language in which the "ghost" is addressed, and the worst problem is with an unclear pronoun reference so that we do not know whether the ghost is making the speaker's house (and life) a medieval "hell" or "purgatory." The difference between the two states is not that clear either. But the poem ends on a strong note of resolve, as the speaker tells the ghost, "I give you until noon" to clear out.

If the first two poems try to come to terms with personal memories, the next five deal with broader cultural experiences— experiences which obviously don't hold much redemptive value for Kees. The first seems to be a rejection of any salvational scheme, whether religious or political. Here the cultural references are clear, with both Christ and Rousseau being invoked. Both figures are in sad shape, however. Rousseau's predictions about the future of man have proved wrong, as the speaker describes "ruined travellers in sad trousseaux" who "roost on my doorstep." It is not just marriages or travelers who are ruined, however; the whole world is in bad shape. Even if the travelers, the speaker speculates, are waiting to be born, they have picked a world of horror and terror. A world in which even the midwife is contemplating suicide.

One of the travelers since deceased turns out to be "one poor hackneyed Christ." "Sad bastard," the speaker muses, "croaking of pestilence." Of course, Kees, in making Christ a twentieth-century traveler, is once again employing Eliot's mythic method. But in Kees the buried gods stay buried. This Christ had been placed in the basement and "has not as yet arisen." Nevertheless, since he is still a curiosity, the speaker intends to sell tickets for those wishing to see the body. "Justice and virtue, you will find," our speaker says in the last and most devastatingly cynical line of the poem, "have been amazingly preserved." The syntax and tone of the sentence suggest a happier meaning, but then the tone of the rest of the poem reinforces something else, and the last word eventually is seen as an undertaker's term: justice and mercy are just as dead as this hackneyed Christ. In one poem, Kees has managed to demolish both the sentimental optimism of Rousseau and the consolation of Christianity.

In the next poem he turns to the more humanistic optimism engendered by the Western tradition or cultural memory. The poem begins appropriately with an image of loss or dwindling:

> As water from a dwindling resevoir [*sic*]
> Uncovers mossy stones, new banks of silt,
> So every minute that I spend with you reveals
> New flaws, new features, new intangibles.

There is deliberate ambiguity in this bittersweet tone. Despite the revelation of new flaws, and despite the dislogistic comparison to a dying reservoir, the tone is essentially complacent, if not honorific. It is as if the poet is emphasizing that it is human to love or admire someone despite imperfections.

But more is at stake than mere interpersonal relationships; for the woman being addressed has a sad voice like one of Eliot's cosmopolites in the *Waste Land,* forlorn and yet with a consciousness that it is the fate of Europe that is making her that way. "I spent that summer in Madrid," she reminisces, "the winter on the coast of France. . . ." and goes on to name mutual friends who were there as well. Doubtless the "that" refers to a summer before the war; now all she can see is the end of an era: "My work has perished with the rest / Of Europe, gone, all gone. We will not see the end." This plaintive weltschmerz, of course, has become a historical judgment. That is, it is traced not to the peculiar psychology of the individual but to the objective historical situation. "End" is again ambivalent. It could refer to the slow decay of Europe as a civilization or the faster end of armed conflict. In the same manner, "work" is left undefined. It could mean works of art that invariably are sacrificed in a war, or it could mean some imaginative or intellectual project that requires a settled and assured order for its support.

The poem then returns to the personal as the speaker of the first lines tells us the woman said goodbye and that her "perfume / Lingered for hours." At first it reminds him of "summer dying there," then the odor becomes "rank and sharp." The usually gradual blending of summer into fall, in other words, becomes the sharper and more distressing odor of sudden and inexorable death. But unpleasant though it is, both as a reminder of the end of a personal relationship and the end of a civilization, it is still a memory of something that was once grand. And so, the narrator tells us in the last line of the poem, he did not air the room.

The fifth variation is more concerned with a different sense of the past, one that the poet has far less use for. Again, the speaker is addressing another, though whether the "you" is male or female is neither certain nor important. The poem is full of conventionally nostalgic details and of suggestions of nostalgic role playing or wish fulfillment. Naturally enough it is that sense of nostalgia that the poet is attacking. The person addressed is handled very sarcastically, as the first stanza sets the tone of his or her "grand entrance" among the "Victorian beadwork" and other bric-a-brac. But though the person enters with a look which would have served "for Pliny or the Pope," the effect is not what might have been desired. Indeed, not only is Pliny not around, but time has taken its toll of even the person's personal acquaintances. If one lives in the past, he will simply be surrounded by photographs of friends with "outmoded smiles." Of all Kees's views of the past, this is the most severe, the one without a single drop of pity or compassion.

The sixth variation has again to do with history, but with a kind not harmful or useless in itself but one that leads to self-deception. What Kees, as a son of the plains states, has in mind is a sense of what is often grandly called "The American Experience," a sense of the voices and examples of our ancestors. "Signboards commemorate their resting place," he begins the poem, and the sentence, at first seemingly blurred and indistinct, soon springs into meaning. "Place" is singular, "commemorate" is used instead of "mark," and signboards instead of "tombstones" because Kees wants to insist, either literally or figuratively, that these ancestors are "graveless." The new society has sent "idiot highways" over their dust. But despite our mistreatment of them, they still speak to us, still help us formulate, in this "parched and caking land"—an image out of the Depression dustbowl—our values and our goals. The problem is that the voices come through distorted. As we re-create them—and hence re-create their experience—they become voices "polished and revised by history," with "martial note[s]" and "words framed in capitals." And so the poet, in order to avoid this distortion and its threatening pomposity and bellicosity, concludes that it is better to be "deaf in a deafening time," a time which he now returns to *The Waste Land* to describe "the sky gone colorless, while the dead / Thunder breaks, a cracked dish, out of the mind." Even that part of our past which is beneficial and available is rendered useless by the perversity of modern culture.

Continuing his pessimistic train of thought, the poet now turns to another possible area of redemption—that of art. Art could be beneficial if it could link past and present by conveying some authentic meaning from the artist, from the work. Kees was to become art critic for the *Nation* and an abstract-expressionist painter in his own right, and the seventh variation shows a great deal of facility in describing the effect of a work of art. If he is not entirely successful, it is probably because he is trying to do too many things at once. For one thing, he is trying to describe the visual effect a work of art has both as a result of the painter's techniques and of the way it affects the environment and the viewer's stream of association. He is also trying to work in some aspects of the painter's life. Finally, he is trying in desperately cynical fashion to comment in terms of absolute value on the futility of both the effect of the work of art and the life of the painter.

An indication of the kind of problem this ambition gives rise to can be seen in the first stanza:

> The eye no longer single: where the bowl,
> Dead in the thickened darkness, swelled with light,
> Transformed the images and moved the artist's hand
> Becomes a framework for our mania.

The shift in tenses is puzzling, and the "eye" has no obvious owner. Furthermore, the bowl seems to be the image in question, yet it also seems to be the subject of "transformed." What Kees is probably trying to do here is to insist that the eye of the beholder, upon seeing the painting, observes not only the painting as technique, but converts it into a commentary on the mania of the day. The next stanza lets us know that the painting must have been done some time ago, but the first elliptical sentence ("And haunts the stairway.") is still present tense, indicating that he is still talking about viewing. The "haunting" is a product of the staying power of the portrait, the way it hangs in our minds. But meanwhile "friends depart" from the room where the painting is hung, "saying goodnight, and carrying their view / Of grapes the model ate in Paris years ago." Now we know that the painting was not only of a bowl, but also of a model and some grapes.

The next couplet is equally enigmatic: "Blue in the morning, green some afternoons; / The night, ambiguous, forgets the signature." "Signature" could easily refer to the painter's signature on the canvas which manages to get lost in the night and the passage of time, but the first line is again without clear reference.

The semicolon following afternoon would seem to separate it
from the following line—it probably refers back to the grapes,
which shift their color under the differing effects of sunlight.
But again, if so, Kees is trying to blend the formal aspects of
the painting with his more cautionary reflections on the ultimate
worth of such enterprises.
    The rest of the poem is less problematic:

> The dust in attics settled and his stove
> Grew cold. About the model nothing much is known.
> It ends the wall and complements the view
> Of chimneys. And it hides a stain.

Here again Kees is combining a lament on the fate of artists
with a comment on the value of art. And his comment on the
modifying effect that an objet d'art has on the natural scene
through a window is coupled with the devastatingly cynical last
sentence of the poem. Art is ultimately simply functional at
the most uninspiring level. One might say that this is a comment
that only the most hopeless philistine or a massively depressed
artist could make. Kees, one suspects, was one of the latter
from time to time.
    The last poem in the series strikes a completely different note.
Of all the variations it is most like a conventional sonnet. The
first two lines, for example, sound almost archaic, or at least
like the work of a modern Petrarchan sonneteer, such as Edna
St. Vincent Millay: "And when your beauty, washed away /
In impure streams with my desire. . . ." The studied abstractions
of "beauty" and "desire" invoke the tradition of the love sonnet,
and the very form of the sentence leads one to suspect that a
compliment to the beloved is to be the eventual payoff. The
enigma comes in the sestet as well. (Kees is perverse enough
to transpose the usual sonnet order—the sestet comes first, followed by the octave.) When the beloved's beauty, the poet
goes on to say, is "only topic for ill-mannered minds," soaked
in the problems of the day, then "Let ruined weather perish
in the streets / And let the world's black lying flag come down."
One would think the poet would shout imprecations on those
ill-mannered minds who make a topic of the departed lovers,
but Kees's language obviously suggests he wants an end not
to the minds but to the world's nastiness.

And, in fact, that is what he does mean, for in the next stanza he insists that only in extraordinary times, years without "Spring," could a mind be disturbed by "ruined weather" when it turns "to you again as you are now. . . ." And then the poem closes with a four-line description of the beloved:

> Tired after love and silent in this house.
> Your back turned to me, quite alone,
> Standing with one hand raised to smooth your hair,
> At a small window, green with rain.

This touching, personal, and obviously felt description of a loved one is surely unique in Kees's work, as is, of course, the feeling that romantic love—even the honest memory of it—can in some way change the world. Thus not too much can be made of it. If just because neither poet can find much else in the past to put his hope in, the poem reminds one of Matthew Arnold's "Dover Beach" ("Ah, love, let us be true to one another"). But Kees's hope, one hastens to add, did not stay there, and one is inclined, given the rest of Kees's output, to wonder how it ever came to be there. A possible answer is suggested by the dedication page of this volume. *The Fall of Magicians* is inscribed "For Ann"—the name of Kees's wife. Perhaps the poem was his gift to her.

Villanelles

Another ambitious series by Kees in *The Fall of Magicians* is "Five Villanelles." This series is also indicative of Kees's burgeoning interest in imitating formal verse patterns, patterns which by and large are highly artificial and constrained in form and development and originate in either Italian or French poetry. A villanelle is a complicated French form, consisting of nineteen lines made up of five three-line stanzas (tercets) followed by one four-line stanza. It uses only two rhymes, and the poem should rhyme *a b a a b a a b a a b a a b a a b a a*. The first line is repeated as lines six, twelve, and eighteen; and the third as lines nine, fifteen, and nineteen. Thus in a nineteen-line poem, eight of the lines are refrain. Kees holds to this pattern except in the first villanelle where he introduces a third rhyme.

Obviously with such an artificial form, one would expect the virtuosity of the poem to take precedence over any depth of meaning or over any real emphasis on content. But Kees has nevertheless managed to keep his characteristic tone and to show himself as a serious poet with a serious and perhaps mordant comment to make. Of course, the sheer amount of verbatim repetition assures that there will not be much chance for twist or development, so that the poem can be dealt with fairly quickly.

The first villanelle—the only one to introduce a third rhyme— is one of Kees's better expressionistic efforts. Here is the first tercet:

> The crack is moving down the wall.
> Defective plaster isn't all the cause.
> We must remain until the roof falls in.

The second line sets up the metaphoric possibilities for the crack, makes it possible for the damage to become a sign of decaying time or impending doom, and the third line reinforces the help-lessness of the onlookers. The rest of the poem plays very cleverly with these possibilities.

The second villanelle is reminiscent of Kees's "June 1940," where he laments the belligerence of former pacifists. "Men we once honored," goes the first line of the villanelle, "share a crooked eye." And the rest of the poem simply reiterates the helplessness of the "we" to change this moral aberration or even to explain it.

The third poem is perhaps the most satiric poem Kees had yet published. It is a biting, scathing attack on publishers and, not unexpectedly, depicts the artist as an alienated and misunderstood outsider. It is the only one separately titled: "A villanelle for the publisher who rejected ———'s book." The poem is not only dedicated to the publisher but addresses him:

> Stiffen your features at any thing new:
> Of all things you do, you do that best.
> From your snug vantage point I scarcely like the view.

Kees continues to pour scorn on the publisher and alternately to quote him to the man's misfortune. "We're liberal here, we welcome every hue / But not the strange, unfashionable, or the obsessed," he has the publisher say. And then, finally, the publisher brags about having turned down Joyce: "He, like so many these days, just befouled his nest." Whether Kees had an actual publisher in mind is unknown, but Joyce's struggles to overcome the timidity and poor taste of publishers on both sides of the Atlantic had already made him a modern artist-hero. In the quatrain, Kees, still scornful and dripping sarcasm, promises to pin a "dime-store medal" on the publisher's chest for his contributions to literature. Again, the intricate form hardly gets in the way of the satiric effect.

The last two villanelles are both about war. The first (the fourth of the series) is not tied down to any specific time or place but in a fairly surreal fashion tries to extract horror from a specific situation. Guests seem to be imprisoned in their house (and cut off from their opium: they can't escape into forgetfulness) while outside no sound can be heard "except the beating of a drum." They know it is the sound of war, but that meaning is too simple. They yearn for a message; they yearn for "noise with complexity," but both are denied them and, the poem implies, will always be denied them. Thus they are locked into a world where nothing can be distinguished but the absurdly simple and meaningless sound of war. In part, the poem obviously functions as a definition of a certain kind of modern hell.

The last is more directly related to the battleground, and its effects come not from surreal or fantastic manipulation but from the real ghastliness of war. It is much like one of the many poems by Wilfred Owen or others realistically describing the horror of war. In this villanelle, for example,

> The major fell down on the blackened lawn
> And cried like a fool: his face was white. . . .

But the overall effect is still more macabre than Owen's because the universe is absurd. The third line (necessarily repeated three times later) is "The truce was signed, but the attack goes on." The line not only underscores a more absurdist view of war but makes the poem more open to symbolic or metaphoric interpretation.

Social Satire

Kees was not without satiric voice in his first volume; and in his second he continues to develop this vein in several poems of unequal merit. "Crime Club," for example, is much like "The Situation Clarified" in *The Last Man,* in which Kees parodies a popular convention in order to comment on the metaphysical uncertainties of the age. The poem begins with a description of what the crime—a murder—is not. There are no conventional clues, no conventional suspects, only a quite dead body in a routine suburban house and a note reading, "To be killed this way is quite all right with me." Given the lack of moral outrage on the part of the victim and the lack of any real motive, the world of the master sleuth "Le Roux" is going to be drastically disturbed. If there is no point in bringing anyone to justice nor indeed any real operative definition of justice any longer, then there is no real identity left for Le Roux. So the last lines of the poem are devoted to describing Le Roux's loss of self-esteem and descent into insanity. Poor Le Roux, seeing the end of a universe of cause and effect and moral absolutes, sits "alone in a white room in a white gown," screaming of war and the pointlessness of following clues.

The poem is a good example of Kees's transformation of philosophic problems into a commentary on the sorry state of the world. It is also a good commentary on how the angst of one person such as the victim can affect another like Le Roux.

The very title of "A Brief Introduction to the History of Culture," at least when viewed after a quick perusal of the poem, serves as another reminder of Kees's refusal to be seduced by Eliot's notion of the grandeur of the past. The poem is a dramatic monologue spoken by the Italian poet Tasso to a representative of the Inquisition, Monsignor Silvio. In the monologue, Tasso, subservient in all things, agrees to make whatever changes may be necessary in his poem—presumably *Jerusalem Delivered.* The poem is prefigured by an epigraph, which looks as if it might have come from a history of culture:

> *Such was the natural course of decay . . . Tasso bowed*
> *before the mutilation; indeed, professed his readiness*
> *to make every change demanded. . . .*

The epigraph sets the tone for the poem and in its servility predicts painful reading. It is an excellent study of the psychology of the fawning mind. Not only will Tasso comply sufficiently to save his neck, he will even out-censor the censor:

> Those stanzas that conclude
> A canto near the end—although examined, tolerated,
> Almost, one might say, approved,
> By the Inquisitor, I've doctored anyway.

Two other satirical poems, "Report of a Meeting" and "Abstracts and Dissertations," are poems without reverberations—both rather routine attacks on the scientific mind. The first is a mildly humorous account of how an elixir supposed to provide eternal youth is tried out on an elderly lion before a convention of scientists. The poor lion dies anyway, leaving the scientists sorely perplexed. The second is a pastiche of jargon, the likes of which are often seen in scholarly dissertations, language lacking in feeling and incapable of conveying true wisdom or insight. Both poems are readable; "Abstracts" is even interesting because of its implicit comments on the use of language, but neither manages to turn itself into a convincing exploration of the real follies of the modern world.

Not surprisingly, most of the poems in *The Fall of Magicians* are a continuation of Kees's major confrontation with the experience of an alienating world and its effect on the individual and on personal relationships. And, as in his first volume, this thematic concern is explored in forms employing anything from almost literal prose statement to the most bizarre surrealistic effects. The poems below are not chosen because they are completely different from some we have already seen, or because they could not easily be classified according to different criteria. They are selected to demonstrate the presence of a fictive effect in Kees. At one extreme they involve a dramatic encounter between two people, with the poet simply being the authorial presence telling the story, his own personality safely tucked away in the background. At the other extreme are poems in which, at least in part, one can assume that the authorial "I" is meant to stand for the poet himself, for Weldon Kees or at least for Weldon Kees's public poetic voice. But even in these poems, it is clear that the fictive or the dramatic encounter seems to be almost present, even if not central, and one is left wondering how much of the "I" is the voice of the poet, how much a fictional persona.

The Dramatic Exchange

Let us begin at the unabashedly fictive end of the continuum. "The Conversation in the Drawing Room," as its title implies, is a dialogue, more specifically a dialogue between an older, society matron type named Aunt Agatha and her nephew Hobart. The setting and the social class of the participants suggest that this could be a kind of Jamesian vignette, with each line of dialogue redolent with overrefined innuendo and psychological attack. But Kees is using the conventions of dialogue with parodic intent. While their language is refined, their experiences are actually horrific, horrific on Hobart's part in the primary sense. In his paranoia he imagines a spot on the wall growing, animating itself and threatening him. Aunt Agatha's dialogue is horrific only in its total lack of comprehension or sensitivity. In other words, the special horror of her reaction is simply the lack of reaction. In her simultaneous concern for social decorum and mindless flirting with spiritualism, she cannot perceive Hobart's dilemma.

Aunt Agatha inevitably responds to Hobart's ever more frantic attempts to get her to notice the growing menace by either rationalizing it away ("Some aberration of the wallpaper no doubt") or rattling on about joining "a new theosophist group," or the experience of her last seance, or warning Hobart about reading overly disturbing fiction like James's *Turn of the Screw*. When Hobart's horror finally drives him into an epileptic seizure, she calmly, almost absentmindedly, wonders where the maid has left the barbital (an antispasmodic drug) and plans the rest of her afternoon routine:

> It is a beautiful afternoon; I will get up about three-fifteen.
> Everything is blissfully quiet now; I am ready for sleep.

Despite its parodic nature the poem does not amount to much as social satire. But as another of Kees's nightmarish pictures of an individual lost in a terrifying world, it is quite effective.

"Conversation in the Drawing Room" is accomplished without any intrusion of the narrative "I." "Girl at Midnight" has an intrusive narrator, but only as a starting force. "Then walk the floor, or twist upon your bed," the narrator begins the poem, addressing a female protagonist; and soon the character begins, through her first-person voice, to dominate the poem, leaving the narrator with nothing to do. But before the narrator has actuated his character, he manages to create one powerful image which serves as a metaphor for the way anger can be self-reflexive, can hurt the one who generates it more than the ostensible victim. "Twist upon your bed," he tells her, "While bullets, cold and blind, rush backward from the target's eye. . . ."

But, again, such destructive emotion is not aimed at an individual—though the poem is about the woman's failure at love—but at the world which assured the failure. She begins by insisting that she will not "dream that dream again" and then gives some of the disjointed images that have filled her nightmare:

> The snap of rubber gloves; the tall child, blind
> Who calls my name; the stained sheets
> Of another girl. . . .

But even in her nightmares, her lover's face is never clear. And no wonder, since he is obviously beset with a death wish, even to the point of imagining them dying (she is quoting him) "The way deer sometimes do, their antlers locked / Rotting in snow." Nevertheless, she desires him, wants his physical presence, wants "the morning filled with sun." But such desires are to be frustrated, and in the last stanza, despite her resistance to more nightmares, she enumerates what she must dream: images of "cities burned away" and deserted piers and "corrupted" nature. "Love is a sickroom," she concludes, and the imagery is once again that of wartime, once again pushing the source of her despair beyond the personal or psychoanalytical. Just to make the point perfectly clear, Kees has her say "The lie of peace / Echoes to no end," before she finally, and sadly, concludes that love can never return.

"The Heat in the Room" is an incredibly taut vignette of two people simultaneously in love and unbridgeably separated by feelings of distrust and hatred which are never explained. It makes remarkable use of what Eliot calls "objective correlatives"—those actions and objects which symbolize and dramatize with no direct authorial intrusion. The poem opens with a man musing that the storm raging outside makes it a good night to have a crackling fire going. And he is helping the fire by feeding it papers, obviously love letters to the woman who is the other character in the poem. But he simply sees the papers, at this moment, as "testimonials to long plateaus of emptiness."

The woman tries listening to the storm, but can't help reading his action symbolically: "He is burning up both of us. / He is burning up our lives." And the hatred that has come between them keeps her from trying to touch him, even though part of her wants to. Meanwhile, if the violence inside is suppressed, that outside is overt. The lightning outlines "the ragged trees," making them appear closer and more ominously black than before. And the man, as if to ward off any attempt at contact by the woman, sets his face against the fire until it becomes an "orange mask" staring stonily at some obscure point. The tension between the two continues to build. When the fire, which has seemed as if it were dying suddenly "Roar[s] like a white-hot furnace," it proves impossible for the woman to contain herself any longer, and she screams.

The refusal to give the protagonists names, the refusal to speculate on the immediate causes for their hatred and estrangement, even the "universal" symbolism of the storm as background all contribute to our being more interested in this as a typically modern experience than to an interest in individual psychology.

"Death Under Glass," except for two enigmatic uses of the first-person plural pronoun, is also a third-person narrative without direct authorial intrusion. The glass in the title refers to a green house (aptly called "hothouse" in the poem) and the poem is a strictly nightmarish fantasy about a man dying in some metaphoric greenhouse. Paradoxically, the poem is very clear, but the symbolism is somewhat murky or at least uninteresting. That is, the details of his struggle to find moisture and coolness are clear enough, but how they relate allegorically to the struggles that man actually encounters in his progress from life to death are not always apparent. But Kees's peculiar sense of the frustration of life is incontestable. In the last stanza, after the man has already found water only to drop into it over his head, he tries walking under water, "drenched," "bewildered," and "done." He tries once again to gain the "rose" that "mistress, wife, or daughter" has insisted he bring back. But then he gives up, defeated, and drowns. The peculiar irony, of course, is that it was only the other(s) who wanted the rose; he detested them.

The Fictional First Person

Two other poems, "Dynamite for Operas" and "River Song," are written strictly in the first person, but this voice is obviously a fiction not meant to be identified in any way with the voice of the poet. Neither poem manages to emerge completely from obscurity, but the main concern of each is fairly obvious. In the first, the speaker is apparently an opera singer. Why he wishes dynamite for the art form he is associated with is not clear. But Kees does seem to suggest that art can only console or protect us from reality for a while, as the singer discovers. For after his grand tour performing in "melodramas of decay," he finds himself back in his "familiar room again," facing the bleak prospects of reality. If his role playing both off and on stage has made it "hard to touch death," that was only a temporary cessation, and in any event seems more valuable as amnesia than as any really functional cure. Thus at the end, at least not self-deceived, he can insist that he likes his current "emptiness" better than the emptiness of amnesia.

Structured like a dream, "River Song" is more enigmatic. The speaker himself has been hanged or at least exhibited from on high in a public place near the river. But his function—as some kind of totem or hanged god—and his attitude change with each three-line stanza, as does the nature of the river. In one stanza the hanging seems to make him a public hero— the river is "bright blue"—as he "wave[s] like a flag." In another, he seems to have given honor to his family name, but the landscape keeps changing for the worse until finally the river is running with blood and the deceit of war is everywhere. Then the speaker wants to die, but apparently must be left there by the warmongers as if suffering rather than death is to be

his fate. The progression from public good—or at least indifference, since the river is "neutral" at the beginning—to intermina-
ble suffering and exploitation is clear, and Kees leaves the poem
open enough that, like Blake's "Mental Traveller," a number
of experiential patterns can be assigned to it.

Toward the Poet's Voice

With "The Ambassador" and "Sestina: Travel Notes" we
come to poems that seem to involve the poet's less fictional
reflections rather than those filtered through a created character.
Seem is appropriate, for the problem is vexed, and the poems
never become out-and-out confessional. Indeed, "The Ambassador" suffers not only from an overall murkiness but from an
indefinite subject for the second-person direct-address portions.
Is the poet addressing himself or another character? It is hard
to tell. Only the infrequent use of *we* lets one know that the
poet is speaking for himself. The murkiness is once again the
result of Kees's surrealistic tendencies. The poem is obviously
about the nature or formative value of experience, and even
though the reiterated last line of the poem is "This is the way
we learn," it is doubtful if the poem posits that it is possible
to learn anything. Certainly the usefulness—as opposed to the
pain and frustration—of experience is never brought out. Instead
life is seen as a series of nightmarish scenes—hands clutching
for banisters that aren't there, pages being turned in absolute
darkness, visions of perfection that disappear almost instantly
never to reappear. Presumably the ambassadors are the experiences themselves, and the message they bring even terrifies legless beggars on roller skates. If the individual images are clear,
however, the overall import is still ungraspable.

"Sestina: Travel Notes" is another poem that makes no real
attempt to fictionalize the speaker, but the *we* is less ambiguous,
both in contrast to an *I* (hence it is not a royal *we*) and by
the presence of a *you*—someone with whom the experience is
being shared. And the *travel* in the title once again refers to a
journey through life—a journey which the speaker is obviously
intent upon declaring is fraught with more traps for himself,
for others, and specifically for the *you*. But what is truly amazing
about the poem is that it reads, except for the final three-line

envoi, like perfectly civilized prose. This despite Kees's having imitated one of the most complex of French verse forms. It is very difficult to imagine a poem that not only makes good sense (at least on a sentence-to-sentence basis) and avoids tortured syntax when it is under the obligation to use the same six end-words of the first stanza throughout the next five stanzas. (The end-words do not appear in the same order; their placement is varied according to a precise formula.) The envoi, the only part to seem syntactically forced, must contain three of the words on the end, the other three buried inside. If one looks at the six end-words one can pretty much guess what the poem is going to be about: *other, voyage, silence, away, burden, harmed.* Even in the abstract, the words reek of alienation and pain. *Others,* for example, either *warn* one away or are indifferent or are *harmed; silence* engulfs us and washes the past *away,* etc. If the tone of the poem is not crystal clear, it is certainly clear enough to have the reader search for meaning rather than treat the poem as a mere tour de force, and, in fact, it is a triumphant example of Kees's tone.

Unclear Identities

The identity of the narrator of "Routes to Headquarters" is not clear nor is the attitude expressed through the poem free from ambiguity. Perhaps some of the obscurity comes from the terza rima form (three-line stanzas rhyming *aba bcb cdc,* etc.) and its necessity to force rhyme. But the diction is also strange when rhyme is not the issue. The poem is an apparently ambivalent look at the wisdom of the East. The speaker's attitude toward his experience with a guru figure—addressed as "effendi" in the poem—is quite unsettled. The "effendi" is apparently a fraud and a "Beast" and though the tortured times force a search for answers, the answer found yields disenchantment with the guru, a "bland maturity," a "long coma," and "glassy eyeballs [staring] toward the churning sea."

"Xantha Street" has a definite first person speaker who personalizes himself by referring to the actual page number (289) of a book he is reading at the time the reflections come to him. It is perhaps more difficult to assert whether the *you* mentioned later in the poem is addressed to the speaker's alter ego or to another person, though the latter is perhaps slightly more defensible since the pronoun changes to *we* after the *you* is introduced. The sex of the *you*, if another person, remains indeterminate.

In addition to this drama between the *I* and *you* there is the obviously fictive environment of the poem, the sharp contrast between the sealed room and a world outside where terrible things are happening, despite the efforts of the "Authorities" to keep things in order. It is the drama between the speaker and this imaginative horror show outside which really provides the "context" of the poem.

The speaker begins by noting that despite the angels rising to heaven in the book he is reading, the evening (full of despair and anxiety) still comes on.

> Poorly cast in an eighth-rate Grand Guignol
> Where every agonist proclaims his purity
> One's sight grows sharper in the glass. . . .

But the more acute sight does not lead to survival or at least not to the desire for survival. Instead, locked up in his or her room, the *you* of the poem is driven to write "Finished. No more. The end," signing the message frantically, "but proud of penmanship." Kees's urbanity is usually restricted to more trenchant forms of social satire, but here the little touch tends to generate more warmth, as if in admiration for the human qualities the *you* managed to hold onto till the end.

Meanwhile, outside, beasts howl, but "Authorities . . . keep the pavements clean." Despite the heavy irony, Kees seems to admit that the authorities do some good. In the next verse paragraph they "steady rooms this earthquake rocks" and hence every face looks at them. But, in the end, the steadied rooms are still a prison and the indistinct future promised by the authorities is "already frayed." And so the poem ends with the speaker and compatriot staring into the void, "in darkened rooms, toward exits that are gone."

"Poem Instead of a Letter" is perhaps the most successful of these poems in which the poet-persona is speaking to a second person. This time, the identity of the "other" is less ambiguous than in some of the other poems, since the speaker is addressing a friend separated from him by a continent. The work, like so many others, is filled with images of winter and decay. But the friend has apparently accepted the inevitability of this doomed world and is able to achieve serenity with a smile "ripened in catastrophe / And wonderfully ready now for death." He is ready for death because the promise of the past is "threadbare," and because he has watched, metaphorically, "that year" turn to winter and the "fragments of a world" drop to pieces "like a rich bouquet." From the visual image of the bouquet, Kees moves to the olfactory sensation of the smell of the decaying flowers, a smell that pervades the current experience of the speaker and is blown by the "rank wind." Perhaps even "ranker winds" will blow, but this one is bad enough, "false" and "dry." Once more there is no consolation in sight, and all the poet can do to end this very personal poem sent in lieu of a letter is to close with "goodnight, goodnight." But the poet in his loneliness doesn't address the goodnight just to the separate friend but to the alienated environment that the absense of the friend makes all the more real. Hence he also bids goodnight "to strangers, to an empty street"—an ending bound to make the desolation all the more poignant.

Conclusion

Kees's second volume, despite the relative paucity of its new offerings, at the very least shows no slackening of invention or want of talent. In its ambitious tackling of a more extended poetic statement, in "Eight Variations," and in its successful manipulations of formal and artificial verse patterns, it shows Kees striving to be a representative modern poet, one who attempts to make a complex poetic statement without the assistance of discursive rhetoric (the fault, many felt, of earlier long poems) and who practices the twin and seemingly contradictory virtues of sincerity of point of view and a highly disciplined and even deliberately artificial craft. Throughout the whole volume, Kees's special and profoundly alienated world view helps emphasize, in its consistency, that here is a genuine, thoughtful sensibility and not just a mindless, if talented, follower of the fashionable.

Chapter Five

Poems 1947–1954 (1954)

When considering an established poet's latest volume, reviewers are apt to look for signs of "development," "increasing maturity," "new departures," etc. Certainly no reviewer of *Poems 1947–1954*, Kees's third volume, containing forty-two poems, would have had trouble spotting several poems fitting these various advances.[1] Yet the volume could not have appeared to be by anyone but Kees. Just about his only trademark absent from it is the interest in formal verse patterns like villanelles or sestinas. But there are a lot of surprises.

First, and doubtless typical of the time, are a number of poems indicative of how war in the aftermath of Hiroshima suddenly became a gruesome and terrifying obsession. Kees had no military experience but suddenly he did not need any, for war now meant the total destruction of civilization and even of the planet. To one endowed, as Kees certainly was, with a sensibility inclined to gorge on nightmarish images of despair, the possibilities for dwelling on this new vision of destruction were quickly seized, and we shall examine a number of such efforts below.

Perhaps in keeping with this new and pessimistic awareness, there seems to be far more expressionistic (or horrific) imagery in this volume and next to none of the playfully surreal. And it is not only the misfortunes of the race that bother Kees. The collection was published a year before his presumed suicide, and his own mental health is an important and inescapable consideration in poems like "The Clinic," which he dedicates to Gregory Bateson, the author of the "double-bind" theory of schizophrenia.

Kees also chooses this volume to present all but one of his "Robinson" poems. The poems represent a new departure for Kees as he tries to make a cosmopolitan New Yorker the focus of much of the emptiness of modern life.

But what is really new about the volume are the experiments

with longer poems and the new influences on Kees that they reveal. "The Umbrella," for example, is not just somewhat longer (seventy-four lines) than usual, but its real claim to our attention is its different tone, borrowed perhaps from Conrad Aiken, to whom it is dedicated. It is one of the rare moments when Kees can afford to be genuinely playful and urbane without any discordant strings playing in the background.

"A Distance From the Sea" is another long poem, and here the master is, once again, T. S. Eliot. But, as we shall see, it is the Eliot of "Return of the Magi" to which Kees now turns for a relaxed, conversational tone. The poem is a masterpiece of psychological analysis.

But Kees's most interesting success with the longer form in this volume is, in fact, the poem he very possibly considered to be his best, for he placed it first in the volume. It is called "The Hourglass," and it has all the hallmarks of a poem a serious poet would like to stake his reputation on. It is distinctively Keesian, but there is little doubt that he has gone to Eliot once again for his tone. This time, however, it is not the fairly simple and undemanding "Journey" that is his source but the far more complex *Four Quartets.* "The Hourglass" is Kees's masterpiece—not only in its tone, but in its manipulation of symbol, its imagery patterns, its purposeful ambiguity. Kees deserves to be an important twentieth-century poet on the basis of this poem alone.

So, to recapitulate, *Poems 1947–1954* contains much that is new and some that is extraordinarily challenging and successful. There is no doubt that this is the same poet who wrote *The Last Man* and *The Fall of Magicians,* but there is also no doubt that he is a poet capable of growth.

"The Hourglass"

Kees's final volume begins with the most impressive longer poem (190 lines) of his career, "The Hourglass." The poem's syntax does not differ that much from ordinary English speech or prose, but it simply does not *function* the way one expects prose to. Instead, it is structured as only a very modern symbolist work might be. It is essentially a series of reflections or meditations on the nature of time, reflections tied together by recurring images, motifs, and symbols. The associative pattern of the poem—that is, the way in which one image reminds one of an earlier occurrence or of a similar one—makes the reader far more of a participant in the poem than is usually the case, makes him far more responsible for making the poem a rich effort. If evaluation consists of deciding whether a poem has a definitive statement to make and manages to make it in a definitive and orderly if not logical way—then evaluation is impossible in a poem like "The Hourglass." Kees's attitude is often clear enough, but except for the necessary but banal conclusion that time is both psychological and objective, meaning is seldom spelled out. Instead, the reader must extract it from the rich experience of the image or the associative reverberations and connections of the symbol or incident.

The poem begins with Kees seemingly musing on the primordial nature of time. He enumerates a large number of things which time is "not." But since they are all manifestly man-made artifacts designed to remind us of time (maple clocks, tower bells, "Grandfather's old silver Waltham," and a factory whistle) Kees must be trying to say that time is more than these items, more than something simply man-made. It is, instead, in his image, "a shadow on a cave's wall, lengthening." The mention of cave, of course, recalls man's preliterate ancestors and suggests how the consciousness of time has been plaguing man, and the lengthening shadow's being caused by the sun reminds us that it is the universe that is responsible ultimately for the passage of time, not man's imagination.

All of these items, man-made or otherwise, will appear and reappear in the poem.

But Kees now shifts to a definition of a particular word in his second stanza. He avoided the word *watch* in the first stanza by referring to the grandfather's timepiece by its trade name. Now he will define the word without giving *timepiece* as a definition and yet the pun is implicit everywhere as the whole definition is redolent with the marking of the passage of time. The word means "a state of watchfulness, or the act of watching." The night is divided into three or four or five *watches* depending on whether you are Hebrew, Roman, or Greek, a reference that stresses not only the ubiquity of concern with time but moves it from the prehistory of the cavemen into literate times. And again Kees begins to elaborate his motifs, beginning with a nautical definition of *watch* as the crew on duty.

    Change of the crew at port and starboard. Mark
    The face of the stone when the sun goes down.
    And mark particularly your passing face against the glass.
    For in the violent stream, a thing is observed
    And carried away, and another comes in place,
    And it too will be carried away. A plume of steam
    Hisses above the factory, and a thousand
    Ham sandwiches come out of the lunch pails.

The last bathetic image of the steam whistle shows how complex
Kees's art can be in this poem. Its bathos—a good modern
touch—shows how trivial as well as profound time is in its effect
upon us. The whistle connects with the "whistle at noon" he
has already introduced in the first stanza, and the "plume of
steam" is another kind of "violent stream," the image and symbol he has just introduced three lines before.

    Earlier in the stanza, of course, the face of the stone should
be marked (or watched) not only because a piece of landscape
looks different at different angles of the sun but because time
changes stone faces just as surely as it does fleshly ones. And
time, the violent stream, can at least be transcended, if not
overcome, through memory, if we mark well the effects of the
moment.

    Part 2 shifts to a different kind of stream or metaphor. Dusk
is now seen moving in as a tangible presence composed of fog
and "blown like chimney of smoke." What the dusk brings in
is a varied set of reflections on the consequences of time. But
first, the very passing of time itself is noted in a refrain, as
Kees once again picks up the image of the change of the watch
and time's effect on stone: "The crew is changed, the stone's
face / Notched in darkness." Again, Kees's language reverber-
ates in unexpected ways, for the night crew is not simply a
carbon copy of the day, but is made up of nocturnal creatures
such as cats, who help remind us of the daily passing of time.
The cats stalk to the sound of another kind of stream, the night
wind whose moaning evokes far different images than that of
the day.

    But time takes place, at least in part, in human consciousnesses,
and consciousness can re-create the past. From the "tonight"
of the cats' forays, Kees goes back "twenty years ago" to a
more human, if also more desolate scene. The stark and gaunt

scene is opened by the image of "a gooseneck lamp" lowering
"its broken head." Kees's visual sense has supplied him with
an image as dismal as any in an expressionistic film and the
rest of the scene lives up to it:

> . . . a threadbare room
> Where strangers spit out olive pits
> And drink from thumb-smeared jars,
> And a phonograph plays *Sweet Savannah Sue.*

It is difficult to tell how personal this scene is, although its
excessive seediness would seem to make it more emblematic
than autobiographical, but Kees's main thrust is yet to come.
The rug in the room and the faces of the strangers, he tells
us, are "like a palimpsest." A palimpsest is an ancient piece
of parchment that has been erased and written over, sometimes
many times. By restoring the erasures, scholars can make the
palimpsest—an item obviously made in time—yield information
about many different historical periods. Thus, even a scene as
stark and discontinuous as the one Kees has just described is
a product of time and carries the story of its progress through
time with it.

But now Kees moves on to another dusk, one further back
in time, and the scene becomes even more archetypal. In a
primeval image of alienation, "two figures by a lake" turn their
backs on one another to "face their separate dusks." What lies
before them are all the images we have seen already, but they
must face them alone.

Now Kees begins a new verse paragraph, content that
he has introduced the subject in proper empirical fashion, by
listing all the abstract terms that have been used to describe
time.

> Real, True, Empty, Mathematical, Continuous,
> Solar, Galilean, Reversible, Sidereal, Absolute,
> Noumenal, Phenomenal.

But such abstractions are quickly dismissed as Kees points out
a more commonsensical fact. When some "oil gets on the
hairspring" of a timepiece, or when a sundial is vandalized,

man's routine is changed. One doesn't get to work on time, the dog gets his food at a later hour, the theater-goer arrives in the middle of the second act. The practical effects of time on every man, Kees insists, are not dependent on his allegiance to any particular abstraction or school of thought. Then Kees goes on to describe a particular timepiece, specifically an ornate clock in the cathedral of St. Mark's (in Venice). Even it, cleverly enough, is the victim of time, for its dial "used to tell the hours," but is now in disrepair. After describing the ornate display of kings, angels, and Madonna which was once triggered into action to mark the passing hours, Kees reduces the significance of that display to one of his recurring, primitive images—"A shadow slides / Against the cave's wall." No matter how aesthetically pleasing this work of art is, it still transmits the same chilling message. And then in one of the more surreal moments of the poem, the poet situates himself high on a roof, much like the roof of St. Mark's, and watches "the owls march, in solemn file, / Past monuments intent against the dusk and time, / Deserting the metropolis, and wish[es] them well." This doomsday scene will be repeated in the last line of the poem. How the owls expect, in their wisdom, to out-do time is not made clear; perhaps Kees means for us to accept their prescience and mock their hubris at the same time. In any case, in the next line of the poem, set off as a separate stanza, the poet now sees the shadow lengthening not over the cave's wall, but over the whole city.

Part 3 is the most abstractly philosophical rumination on time, the most reminiscent of Eliot's philosophical musing in *The Four Quartets*. The theme of the fifteen line section is announced in the first two lines:

> *Being at the expense of Becoming*
> *Becoming at the expense of Being.*

As the rest of the section makes clear, the inevitability of the world of flux is certainly a mixed blessing, since "Becoming infests all time with instability / And imperfection," yet it is also the key to any kind of perfecting process. We may never reach the perfection of the ideal, but through time we can strive to get closer. So the poet is ready to accept the challenge: "Here, in the rubble, clear a passageway."

But if this section looks to the somewhat impersonal future as all organisms strive to evolve into higher forms, the next section attempts a retreat into the past, a personal past. In a winter landscape, full of the reminders of death, the poet finds himself in the past, "Somewhere, alone." Suddenly he realizes his mind has transported him back to his tenth year. This mental movement into the past serves momentarily as "some immense retreat / Out of the world of men." But eventually, as the recall comes into sharper focus, it only reminds him that even then he was aware of time and afraid of its effects. Standing, in memory, outside his father's door he hears, "Immense and terrible, / The ticking of a clock."

The first line of part 5 provides the apt transition between this depiction of childhood terror and the poet's more recent experience. It is the refrain we have already seen now run together as a single line: "The crew is changed, the stone's face notched in darkness." But no matter how much the poet has changed, he is still terrified by the passage of time. The scene is now in the present in a New York apartment, where poet and lover, "Sheeted," lie at night in bed, watching the shadows of headlights from the street play on their walls. Other sounds drift up too and sleep is impossible. What is possible is dread, feelings of alienation: "It is the time of seconal, of loss, of / Heartbeats of a clock, enormous, by your bed. . . ." And then the shadows of headlights are converted into the shadow that slides around the caves in earlier stanzas. Drawn to the window, all the poet can think about is the passing of time, the dimming of the light—a return to the doomsday reading. But then a noise like that of seeds rattling strikes his ear and a train of associations is set off which tend to make the moment memorable, to make it a "speck in time" that "endures and is not lost." But this personal victory, if that is what it is, this way of keeping time from destroying all of one's life minute by minute is still just a personal, not a cosmic, victory. And Kees closes the poem by describing the clock above the city hall in Prague, a far more somber timepiece than the one at St. Mark's. Here the figure announcing the hours is Death, and the rest of the poem supplies us with images either of death or of new discomforts as when time "shapes the blood of new wounds." And finally, in a cascade of images we have seen again and

again, the poem suddenly turns cosmic and at the same time completely pessimistic as time finally brings about the inevitable: "A planet surges, plunging, and goes out."
This reading only hints at the richness of this poem. It is fitting that Kees's most daring technical effort should be on one of the subjects to which he constantly recurs during his poetry—the meaning and function of the past. It is equally fitting that Kees once again makes the poem typical in his refusal to make his own ego the center of the universe.

The American Landscape

"Travels in North America" is pretty much what its title implies. If the poet cannot achieve any real Whitmanesque enthusiasm for the American landscape, the poem at least conveys a certain delight in variety. It also makes clear that it is a postwar landscape that is being traversed. Los Alamos is on the itinerary, where "tall young men in uniform keep watch" over "The University of California's atom bomb." Naturally, following a journey across country, celebrating cities and monuments one after another, does not lend itself to any sort of rigorous or unusual structuring. But one oddity does present itself—the poet is not describing a journey being taken or recalled from mere memory. Instead the poem is set up dramatically to suggest that the speaker has a map in front of him and is recalling his journey with its aid. The names on the map not only allow him to recall places he actually visited, but those off the route whose entries in guide books caught his eye.
Finally, even a respect for variety vanishes as the speaker is overcome with the "sudden sense" that he has "seen it all before." It is only at the end that the poem becomes more distinctly Keesian, only then that he begins to brood on the significance of journeys:

Journeys are ways of marking out a distance,
Or dealing with the past, however ineffectually,
Or ways of searching for some new enclosure in this space
Between the oceans.

Kees never says which reason motivated his journey. Instead he now locates himself at the shore of the ocean, watching the afternoon waves cast their refuse on the shore. Amidst an extraordinary amount of dead, ruined, and watersoaked debris is a "ragged map, imperfectly enclosed by seaworn oilskin." And now it is this stained and partially indecipherable map, and not the road map used at the beginning of the poem, that receives our attention, as the poet slips further and further away from an actual journey and into reverie and fantasy. For the map brings back the past: first a night ten years earlier in Brooklyn Heights, then he quickly jumps to the west and back again past service stations and Ford assembly plants until he is on the "washboard roads / Of Wellfleet," Massachusetts. After this memory of summer vacation, the poet shifts to the future where he can see, "where you are, and where I am, / And where the oceans cover us." The poem is neither neurotic nor paranoid enough to make us assume that the speaker is talking about either a suicide or a retreat into fantasy à la Prufrock. He may simply be conceding that death is certainly the ultimate destiny of all travelers. One is hard-pressed, frankly, to decide whether this ending does anything for the poem. The first two-thirds of "Travels in North America" are a good workmanlike description of the American experience in some of its gritty particulars. Perhaps the poem should have ended before trying to shift from the shared experience of the landscape to the hidden turmoil or memories of a single psyche.

The Confidence Man

Though its success may be doubtful, "Travels" does mark something of a new departure for Kees, and so does "A Distance from the Sea." Once again, T. S. Eliot is a definite model, but here the poem that comes to mind is "Journey of the Magi," a poem written after Eliot became a Christian. Like that later Eliot effort, Kees's poem is a dramatic monologue, spoken by a quizzical follower of Christ, and done in a modern colloquial tone. If Eliot's hero has too much of a modern sense of the hardships of belief, Kees's hero has no belief at all, simply an admiration for the finesse with which Christ and his followers were able to pull off such phony miracles as walking on water and the resurrection. This is in part self-admiration, needless to say, for the speaker was one of the principal con men. The

poem, then, might be called the gospel according to a political hack.
It is uttered long after the events when the speaker has reached an advanced age. He plunges immediately into a recollection of his proudest achievement:

> That raft we rigged up, under the water
> Was just the item: when he walked,
> With his robes blowing, dark against the sky,
> It was as though the unsubstantial waves held up
> His slender and inviolate feet.

The effect was perfect; the crowd was ecstatic. Surprisingly, despite the cynicism implicit in a "rigged" miracle, the poem is neither cynical nor pessimistic. It is as if Kees, devoid of religious belief, wanted to come as close as possible to the spirit of Eliot's faith. The poem is an honest appreciation of craftsmanship (pride in the way the "miracles" were brought off; admiration of the way Christ handled himself in executing the miracles) and a defense of such rigging in terms of human needs. "Life offers up no miracles, unfortunately, and needs assistance," the speaker insists. And strangely enough, this supplying of a miracle brought not only hope to the masses but a Faustian sense of accomplishment to the perpetrators. "Not out of love, so much, or hope, or even worship, but / Out of fear of death" was the miracle performed. Performing the miracle was like bringing lighted candles into a world of darkness, a world bereft of hope, and watching the candles, "one by one, take fire, flame / Against the long night of our fear." With this power to rig a miracle, "We thought / That we could never die." Ironically the Christian hope of salvation is visited even on the perpetrators of the fraud. And it was a magnificent fraud—of that the speaker is clear. It brought hope to a world sorely in need of it.

This Faustian hubris is really nothing more than the courage to be, the self-appreciation necessary to keep from doubting one's worth. Now in the fullness of time and withdrawn to a mountain far away from the scene of his favorite miracle, the speaker is ready to face the inevitable. He has already spoken of the kind of ecstasy or resignation before the inevitable:

Was it sunlight on the wave that day? The night comes down.
And now the water seems remote, unreal, and perhaps it is.

But if the memory of past accomplishments now seems unreal,
his tone indicates that he no longer has need for such ego-
enhancers. Since he does not have the Christian afterlife to look
forward to, he may not, like Eliot's Magus, actually be glad
of another death; but his tone indicates a serenity before the
inevitable.

Strangely enough, in a poem which (in a sense) debunks
Christianity, Kees was able to project himself into another character deeply enough to shake his own dour pessimism. This is
one of the few poems in the entire canon that cannot be described as morbid or pessimistic in their conclusion.[2]

Delightful Thoughts, Delightful Images

Another poem that is fairly long (seventy-four lines) by Kees's
standards is "The Umbrella," and its dedication to Conrad Aiken
should alert us that it is somewhat atypical of his work. Aiken,
a contemporary and friend of T. S. Eliot, has always been admired but never considered a mainstream American poet. Unlike Eliot's, his poetry does not deal with modern cultural crises.
Instead, Aiken seems far more interested in the harmony of
meter and rhyme, in the aesthetic delight of beautiful images.
It is not that Aiken is devoid of ideas, it is simply a matter of
his poetry insisting on calling attention to other things as well.
"The Umbrella" is a poem full of entertaining and delightful
images suggested by the title. And though the subject may not
seem to be of the utmost significance, obviously any cultural
artifact with a long history can spawn all sorts of anecdotes
and myths. Doubtless most of the "myths" in "The Umbrella"
are solely the product of Kees's imagination, but the effect of
the grand design of the mythic method being used to focus
on something as ephemeral as an umbrella simply contributes
to the charm of the poem.

Kees allows himself an all-knowing narrator—one who can
speak as though he has lived through various epochs and cultures
and can serve as a cultural memory for all. Thus he moves
from the "hot countries" to Buddha, to the building of the

ark of the covenant, using all three as excuses for planting the seed of an elm. But, in grandly surreal fashion, the seed does not sprout a tree, but instead an umbrella with "black spines / Of metal and a tent of cloth. . . ." What follows is a potpourri of anecdotes about umbrellas. Stories about the Mikado rub shoulders with Chinese myths, with accounts of a hunting party led by Queen Victoria's son, with a story emphasizing how a culture can reverse the function of an artifact:

> And when we left the corpses
> Out of doors, we put umbrellas over them,
> Not to shield them from the sun, but rather
> To protect the sunlight against pollution
> By the dead.

The poem, in fact, is so taken with all the lore it generates that even when the poet gets to the present he is unable to return to the more usual Keesian mode. In a storm, with wind pelting the harbor, the poet watches a black umbrella "ripped apart and wrong side out," blown down the beach until a sudden gust of wind lifts it up and out over the water, "flapping and free, / Into the heart of the storm." The word *free* is enough to keep the image from being as morbid or discouraging as the usual Kees effort. Instead we are far enough into the land of ambiguity to concentrate, once again, on the beauty and energy of the image itself.

Murder In a Drug Store

"The Testimony of James Apthorp" is another ambitious attempt, slightly longer (seventy-three lines in four parts) than Kees's usual efforts. Purporting to be based on the interior monologues of a deranged murderer, the syntax and diction are perforce disordered, although all the elements are ultimately forced to make sense. After all, the desired final effect is not the ambiguity and inventiveness within the reader's mind, but an "explanation" of a deranged act. It is typical of Kees that Apthorp's derangement is not totally idiosyncratic or ideopathic. Apthorp reacts to accounts of suicides (one possibly that of a young child) and of an eight-year old girl dying of cancer. The world is not without its objective horrors. Unfortunately for his druggist-victim, Apthorp goes to a pharmacy seeking a cure for these ills amid "the vaseline and aspergum." When the druggist replies, "We do not carry that," Apthorp apparently loses his grip completely and murders him. Kees's powerful and impressively manipulated imagery coalesces so successfully into understandable—if psychotic—patterns that one is torn between admiring the razzle-dazzle of the artist and becoming immersed in sympathetic identification with the speaker.

Aftermath of War

"Travels in North America" took us to Los Alamos, which the speaker duly noted was the home of the atom bomb, and the implications of that catastrophic weapon and the war in which it was first used weigh heavily on Kees's mind in several other poems. Kees still does not acquire an ideological stance. Instead he uses the doomsday possibilities of the bomb and the destructiveness and inhumanity of the war to confirm his general feeling that the problem is not in the individual but in the world around him.

"Dead March," for example, never mentions the bomb, but draws heavily on the horrors of the European war. The title itself tends to show the confusion Kees sees as history. The inclination is to normalize it into "*Death* March," a term well known in the war. But the adjectival *dead* forces one to consider the possibility that the month of the year—the last of winter— is being referred to. If that is so, April with its renewal is nowhere in the poem. But the dead do march through the poem. In fact, the poem opens with an allusion to the marriage of Hitler and his longtime mistress Eva Braun on the last day of their lives:

> Under the bunker, where the reek of kerosene
> Prepared the marriage rite, leader and whore,
> Imperfect kindling even in this wind, burn on.

"Kerosene" refers to the fuel with which their bodies were doused after their suicides. During the preparations for this cremation, "Someone in uniform hums Brahms." The juxtaposition of the barbarism of the Nazis and the glories of Germanic culture disturbed many intellectuals after the war, particularly in its implication that culture—the arts and philosophy—did not necessarily make a person ethically sound. Kees very economically allows the point to be made in five words without comment. After this, the poem becomes both more surreal and expressionistic. Asserting presumably that the past is never dead, Kees has the Holy Roman emperor asleep in a mountain hideout, snoring through seven centuries. Is Hitler now in the Himalayas, he asks. Of course, no one knows where the next Hitler will come from, but Kees manages to make his point that another will surely appear and at the same time wildly satirizes those who assume that Hitler escaped from Berlin and made his way to freedom. Then the poem moves to the heartland of the United States, to "Cleveland or Sioux Falls." But the air over these cities seems as if it were pumped from "Dusseldorf." Even the United States shares in Europe's self-destruction, as does Russia, the country that had become the other great superpower.

But the most economical, imaginative, and horrifying effect of the poem is reserved for the last two lines:"—And not far from the pits, these bones of ours, / Burned, bleached, and splintering, are shoveled, ready for the fields." Perhaps playing the image of Hitler's cremated remains against that of the incinerated bodies of the concentration camp victims says more about the amorality of poetry than some would like to know. The repetition of the imagery does, however, allow the poem to open and close with the smell of burning humanity, and the "ours," as is often the case in such surreal efforts, is ambivalent or ambiguous enough for the reader to include both possibilities—the dramatized voice of concentration camp victims and the voices of all humanity in a world gone crazy. The poem is horrific, and a good indication of how an imagination like Kees's, already tending to see the world as self-destructive, could become even more aghast at future prospects.

"Interregnum" is even more horrific in some ways, certainly in its conclusion. It is composed of four stanzas, each addressed to a different war-time participant—peasant, ambassador, participant-observer, and objector. Each stanza is unmistakably bitter.

The peasant is told to engage in class warfare ("Butcher the evil millionaire") and then told to "drill your hogs and sons for another war." The juxtaposition of hogs and sons suggests the essential doltishness of the peasant, his inability to see how brutish his behavior is. The ambassador is essentially charged with hypocrisy, the participant as gullible beneath all his "medals from the time before." Given this attitude, one would think that the objector would come in for praise, and perhaps he does. But if so, it is remarkably bitter praise:

> Hide in the dark alone, objector;
> Ask a grenade what you are living for,
> Or drink this knowledge from the mud.
> To an abyss more terrible than war
> Descend and tunnel toward a barrier
> Away from anything that moves with blood.

That the objector is living a less than human life, an alienated life, is not surprising, nor would it be surprising for Kees to praise him for the moral courage that it takes to choose such a life. But that does not seem to be what is happening here. Instead, the objector is removing himself from all earthly life and propelling himself toward some void even worse than war. Kees leaves us with the suspicion that, like many of the pacifists of the 1930s, his commitment to conscientious objection was modified by the course of events in the early 1940s.

Survivors

Three other poems seem to be about survivors of war or nuclear holocaust. "The Locusts, The Plaza, The Room," for example, is spoken by a man who seems to be the only survivor of a war, although it is possible he is simply locked in his own mind, driven crazy by events. He and his mistress lived through atrocities, natural calamities, sabotage, and even "made love while bombers roared on by." But now she is "dead with the rest," the locusts are gone, and he is turned into something of a catatonic.

"Equinox" is more explicit. As the final line informs us, the poem is about "the last survivor of the race." The last survivor turns out to be an old woman with "rind" for skin and bald as a "melon" (signs of radiation sickness?) who lives in a remote village which has seen its weather go from semitropical to wintry and snow-covered (another sign of nuclear disaster). Although the woman may indeed be suffering from radiation sickness, Kees may have clouded the issue more than he intended to. She suffers from "paresis," a generalized paralysis that is one of the indications of tertiary syphilis. Perhaps he is trying to suggest that this condition can also result from an overdose of radiation. In any case, it is clear that the rest of the race has disappeared, and the woman's syphilis could hardly have been responsible for that.

"Speeches and Lyrics for a Play," has its last-survivor theme as well, although in form it is reminisicent of Kees's earlier fragmentary drama, "A Cornucopia for Daily Use." Eliot does not seem to be much of an influence on this later dramatic effort, however. Indeed, one of the songs assigned to the chorus is a parody of Blake's "The Tiger":

> Geiger counter, clicking soon,
> In the forests of our noon,
> What immortal eye will glimpse
> These corpses, and our impotence?

Anyone with the original in mind will grit his teeth at this travesty's loss in power and rhythm, but the mention of the instrument used to measure the presence of radiation is indicative of Kees's postwar awareness.

The survivor theme occurs in the last "speech" when two children, "rummaging in the debris of a destroyed building" find a fragment of a letter and read it. It is from a man to his loved one, and amid signs that perhaps a nuclear war has taken place, the man speculates that creation has ceased. In any case, he obviously feels his own death approaching. But again, Kees manages to undercut the last-survivor theme. The presence of children suggests that all creation has not ceased, but even more important for Kees, it has not ceased to be perverse either. The last lines in the work are stage directions, and in them we learn that the "child crumples the letter into a ball and tosses it into the debris." Mankind, even those who have seen the debris, will neither learn from the letter nor extend sympathy to its author. The more things change. . . .

The Clinical Experience

Despite Kees's involvement with psychoanalysis and what must have been the growing sense of despair that was to drive him to contemplate suicide, few of the poems are about mental illness per se, and only two—"The Clinic" and "The Furies"— are possibly about a personal situation. While these differ considerably, both are alike in resolving themselves in an unexpected and even cynical way.

"The Clinic" is dedicated to Gregory Bateson, the anthropologist and inventor of the "double-bind" theory that has become very influential in defining schizophrenia. As noted in chapter 1, Kees helped Bateson make the film "Three Families" to illustrate the theory. The poem is about a mental health ward and begins by showing a "delusion" or metaphoric excess on the part of the speaker as he describes the clinical torturing of cats. When the doctor turns the current on,

> I am caught
> With all the other cats that howl
> And dance and spit. . . .

After the experimentation is over, he goes home with a milligram of calcium chloride (more frequently used as road salt) applied directly to his brain and goes to sleep.

But sleep is not a cure and the center of the poem is devoted to a search for reasons and mockery—much like several poems in *The Fall of Magicians*—of scholarly behavior. Dr. Edwards keeps records of sixteen patients but cannot find causes or explanations. One is encouraged to read certain authorities on the "hypoplastic heart," which would seem to mean the shriveled heart, the possible cause of all our problems. The speaker follows the scholarship in the "dark backward" seeking for answers, but only becomes more terrified, only generates more frightening apparitions and illusions:

> And then we came into that room
> Where a world of cats dance, spat, and howled
> Upon a burning plate.—And I was home.

It is this ending, in which a certain kind of insanity becomes the familiar and even the norm that ties "The Clinic" with "The Furies." The latter opens with an allusion to a passage in *The Waste Land* and to its ultimate source, the biblical account of the risen Christ on the road to Emmaus: "Not a third that walks beside me, / But five or six more." But these spectral figures are not harbingers of the truth of the resurrection, as Christ was, nor of the redeeming vision that will lead us out of the wasteland, but are instead the creatures of a nightmare, all described in terms that would do a mediocre horror film proud. They have associations with—and hence their genesis in—the poet's past, as the best lines in the poem make clear. One of the figures is a cripple,

> Whose crutches shriek on the sidewalk
> As a fingernail on a slate
> Tears open some splintered door
> Of childhood.

The speaker lives a frightful life with these demons and can only exorcise them when absolute fatigue drives him to sleep. There he can dream of their death. Yet he knows that like doctor or wife, his demons always keep a watch around his bed, "possessors and possessed," and paradoxically are the "protectors of [his] life." The "dark backward" in the "The Clinic" took the speaker not just into the scholarly archives searching for an answer but into his personal past. It is not unusual for Kees to emphasize the importance of the past. But he has never gone so far, as in these two poems, in emphasizing the necessity of the past even if that past is totally horrific.

Other Uses of the Past

Kees still admired Eliot's juxtaposition of past and present, although, as expressed in "The Speaker," he thought Eliot tended to gild the past. Now he found a way to use the facts, voices, and lore of history and draw on its richness without getting caught in nostalgia. Perhaps "way" should be plural, for the technique does vary. What remains constant is the lack of gilding. "The Lives" and "Round," for example, exemplify one way of assimilating such knowledge without exaggerating its significance as a norm for the present. The former is an exercise in historical trivia:

> "History is a grave and noble pageant," Landor said.
> His family life at Gherardesca proved impossible.
> In 1844 his daughter gave him Pomero, a dog.

This juxtaposition of chatty personal history with Landor's formal declaration makes that declaration look more vapid than perhaps it really is. The rest of the poem supplies other facts about Landor and other nineteenth-century figures (Mrs. Browning, Professor Norton, Santayana, Nietzsche, Booth Tarkington), facts trivialized by their lack of proper or customary context. After returning to Landor and allowing him to repeat his definition of history and then change it to "stately pageant," the poem closes with the only survivors of that epoch:

> On the neglected lawn, the iron dogs and the deer,
> Rusted among the weeds, alert, indomitable, keep watch.

In *The Waste Land* Eliot speaks of the "fragments" of that poem as being objects to "shore against my ruin." Kees's fragments are not going to protect him from chaos, nor will they correct the unalterable fact that objects without feelings survive us. Finally, of course, in this less than perfect world, even those objects will be gone: after all, they have already started rusting.

"Round" may seem to allude to a traditional verse form. It does not, but it does describe Kees's mode of operation. Almost every item gets repeated, and the first and last lines of the poem are the same. Especially since so much is repeated later, the first stanza will give a good approximation of the whole:

> "Wondrous life!" cried Marvell at Appleton House.
> Renan admired Jesus Christ "wholeheartedly."

> But here dried ferns keep falling to the floor,
> And something inside my head
> Flaps like worn-out blind. Royal Cortissoz is dead,
> A blow to the *Herald-Tribune.* A closet mouse
> Rattles the wrapper on the breakfast food. Renan
> Admired Jesus Christ "wholeheartedly."

Renan is the nineteenth-century author of *La Vie de Jesu.* Royal Cortissoz was the art critic for the New York newspaper mentioned. It is doubtful that Cortissoz was nearly as important as Renan, whose work was part of the last century's tradition of skeptical Biblical scholarship. But the two bounce against one another along with information about Andrew Marvell and the author's problems with his head and household pests. One wonders if something has not been learned from Joyce as well as Eliot. When everything gets caught up in the associative patterns of the mind, everything becomes equally trivial or equally capable of leading to trivia. Here the pattern is rather formal, as if dictated by extrinsic rules, and not associative, but the effect of the juxtapositions is the same. The knowledgeable man is simply one with a broader grasp of the absurd.

If these two poems deal with facts and quotations from the past, "Testimonies" and "A Late History" consist in large part of invented voices from the past, voices designed to sum up the collective attitude of a historical epoch.

"Testimonies" consists of five different voices, each of which describes the period in which he lives and says something about his relationship with God. The first voice is a good example of the procedure followed:

> I baited bears and prayed. The Queen
> Grew inky on Boethius. Between
> The angels and the animals we lived and died.
> The sun, the King, and my own being blazed one.
> I spoke occasionally to God.

The voice comes to us from the Middle Ages—as the reference to Boethius implies—and the speaker, despite his violence, is obviously close to God, can even speak to God. The next two voices have something of the closeness, though the second is a Jew who has been deserted by God and subjected to massacres,

and the third is a knight who has been denied a vision of the
Grail, has seen a fellow quester dying, and has also seen some
of his soldiers visited with the vengeance of the Lord in the
form of "spongy growths" in their mouths. The growths are
excised and placed upon the coals as a form of sacrifice. God
is near in all three, if not always amicable.

But the fourth voice is from the eighteenth century, probably
that of a starving writer. (He mentions Grub Street, the traditional address for hacks.) This speaker can only apprehend God
in a slogan. In the midst of general famine and his own destitution, all he can say is, "God save the King, the Army, and
the House of Lords!" With the fifth voice, we are in modern
urban America. Instead of describing some specific action of
the speaker, the voice is reduced to a simple and plaintive, "I
live." And amidst the crowds on the elevated railway, the
speaker finds Christ—"a red-cheeked, chromo" representation
"Hung with the bloody calves' heads in the butcher shop."

Perhaps in this one poem, Kees does adopt Eliot's view of
the shabbiness of the present when compared with the past.
The modern Christ, far from being a god with meaning or
terror for man, is not even a proper hanged god of myth any
more. He has simply become another slaughtered animal in a
butcher shop. And bereft of godhead or presumably the ability
to have faith in anything, man is reduced to exulting in his
mere existence, as if any more notable accomplishment were
clearly beyond him.

"A Late History" is perhaps the most enigmatic of these
poems. It is in four sections, with the first three plain enough
in their way. Despite some realistic detail and the speaker's
ability to look at present, past, and future time in the same
breath, the speaker or speakers are obviously recalling present
moments from the past. The first is a follower of Newman,
the second, a Victorian enjoying a reunion in honor of the
poet Rossetti; the third, a personal recollection of a painter
who sounds suspiciously like Toulouse-Lautrec. The occasions
are happy enough, but each is marred by the incorporation of
a future event—that is, a happening which takes place after
the moment being recorded. Newman is unmasked, horrible
old age overcomes all in the second part, and the painter commits
suicide. It is the fourth part that proves enigmatic. The speaker

tries to shift from a "then and later" framework to a present-tense "now": "Now, now, if ever, love opening your eyes, / The great blind windows lifted toward the sun, the doors / Thrown open wide." But note that this is not a sentence and that what is to happen now, if ever, is not made clear. Instead the speaker immediately lapses into a prediction about the immediate future. "Soon, soon, these closings start. . . ." Presumably he means the closing of the items that have just opened in the lines before. But when these closings do happen, the speaker suddenly finds himself locked in the present: "Now, Soon, and Later have become / Each other, . . . Do I wake or sleep? It is as late tonight as it will ever be."

Obviously the poem is rich with interpretive hints. Perhaps the narrator is being forced to live completely in the present, but if so the instrument of that force is not evident. And perhaps he is about to die, but there is no reason for his mind not to wander back and forth in time, even in his last minutes. And perhaps the answer to his question in the last line is that he is sleeping and some special logic of a nightmare is forcing itself upon him. Whatever, the poem ultimately succeeds as provocation.

Reminding one in some ways of Kees's early "Insectae Borinquensis," where he constructs a mythology about an insect intent upon destroying the earth, "A Pastiche for Eve" calls on all kinds of lore—Christian, classical, and modern—to come up with a tribute to Woman. As one would expect, Kees feels free to ignore chronological time in this "eternal" portrait, so the brew can become especially unsettling at times:

> While warming up the beans,
> Miss Sanders broods on the Rhamnusian, the whole earth
> worshipping
> Her Godhead. Later, vegetables in Athens.
> Chaste in the dungeon, swooning with voluptuousness,
> The Lady of the Castle weds pure Christ, the feudal groom.

The next stanza begins with a reference to Swift's well-known disgust with women's alimentary functions. Then the poem comes round finally to a linking of man and woman—"Their pain, their blood, are ours."

Robinson

The only enforced continuity among a group of poems in Kees's canon exists in the so-called Robinson poems. There are four poems, one of which appeared in *The Fall of Magicians,* the other three in his last volume. All have as their protagonist a man named Robinson. One immediately thinks of Robinson Crusoe, and perhaps the analogy is just. Robinson Crusoe was cut off from the rest of humanity by geography. Our modern hero is cut off from the rest of humanity by his solipsistic perception.

The first poem to appear was simply called "Robinson." Kees does not attempt to make Robinson unique; instead Kees seems to be more interested in the quality of a solipsistic mind. Indeed, the poem seems to suggest the inevitability of solipsism:

> The dog stops barking after Robinson has gone.
> His act is over. The world is a gray world,
> Not without violence, and he kicks under the grand piano,
> The nightmare chase well under way.

The masculine pronouns refer to the dog—Robinson is noted only by his departure. If one interprets this stanza in a manner consistent with the apparent thrust of the rest of the poem, then the real meaning of the first line has to do with the absence of the dog's existence after Robinson has left. That is, the poem seems to be about the way that Robinson's world exists only in Robinson's head. But the rest of the stanza, concentrating on the dog's nightmare, seems to be the kind of detail Kees could not resist—even dogs are caught up in the terror—but it would certainly lead a casual reader to suspect that the dog was the real subject of the poem. The second stanza gets the poem back on track:

> The mirror from Mexico, stuck to the wall,
> Reflects nothing at all. The glass is black.
> Robinson alone provides the image Robinsonian.

What Robinson sees reflected in the mirror is a self-image and an image of his immediate world, which the rest of us simply cannot see. This is not to say we cannot see the objects themselves:

> . . .walls, curtains,
> Shelves, bed, the tinted photograph of Robinson's first wife,
> Rugs, vases, panatellas in a humidor.
> They would fill the room if Robinson came in.

But without Robinson and the special associations he brings to the objects, they remain simply an enumeration of particulars. And the next two stanzas play on the disparity between object and the special meaning which inhabits only one mind.

The other three Robinson poems appeared scattered throughout *Poems 1947–1954.* "Aspects of Robinson," which appears first, is perhaps the easiest of all the Robinson poems to discuss. Appropriately, this poem is devoted to Robinson the public man. Thus Robinson is seen "at cards at the Algonquin," taking cabs around Manhattan, standing on a rooftop in Brooklyn Heights, buying a copy of the *Times.* Of course, he is not always debonair; he is sometimes "afraid, drunk," sometimes in bed "sobbing" with "a Mrs. Morse." But such items are a minor key, for in this poem Robinson at least has the appearance of success. But Kees knows otherwise and saves the last line to show something more of the real Robinson. After describing Robinson's sartorial taste and his fashionable accessories, Kees points out that they are "all covering / His sad and usual heart, dry as a winter leaf." The line, however, is too easily moralistic and jars with the polish and élan that Robinson has and with which Kees brings off this description of a man about town. But neither the heart nor the end of the poem bears much relation to the Robinson we have already seen in the first poem.

When we turn to the next poem, "Robinson at Home," we seem to be dealing with another "aspect." For here it is not Robinson the debonair, but Robinson the solitary, unresponsive to the sounds and odors of spring, refusing to respond to the symbolism of renewal, strangely passive and feverish at the same time. The passivity is simply recorded:

This sleep is from exhaustion, but his old desire
To die like this has known a lessening.
Now there is only this coldness that he has to wear.

The coldness would seem to have come in with the previous winter, and this might be the same man we have seen earlier but now more withdrawn from the world. In his nightmares, Robinson is unsure of his own identity and assigns all sorts of roles to himself, from scholar to beggar to confidant of popes. But he cannot find an authentic self in what he calls "this madhouse that I symbolize" and wakes only to silence—a deafening silence: "It drones like wires far beyond the roofs, / And the long curtains blow into the room." The hope of spring is apparently still on the wind disturbing Robinson's curtains, but there is no sign that he will respond to it. Instead the silence of the void seems to be overwhelming. In "Relating to Robinson," the last of the group, Robinson has deteriorated even more, has left his nightmarish bed to roam the streets, describing his awful visions to passersby.

But the more interesting technical point about the last poem is that the emphasis is really not on Robinson but on the narrator. The poem is about the narrator's seeing Robinson—or "someone else"—in the deserted New York street on a summer night. In other words, the narrator's confusion is at the heart of the poem. Whether Robinson or not, the effect is still eerie. Whoever it was had "dilated, terrifying eyes / That stopped my blood." What Robinson has to say is slightly manic but not really threatening. Nevertheless, it terrifies the narrator, who bolts:

> Running in sweat
> To reach the docks, I turned back
> For a second glance. I had no certainty,
> There in the dark that it was Robinson
> Or someone else.

Obviously, by this poem, the horror has superseded Robinson, and the narrator has been affected by it, whether Robinson was on the scene or not. (It is possible that the whole encounter is simply the hallucination of a deranged narrator.) And the poem closes by contrasting the peaceful, if garish, New York street scene with the narrator's own emotions. Thus Robinson makes his exit, playing second fiddle to a stronger and more central character.[3]

Remaining Poems

Of the remaining poems in the volume, few offer many surprises. A handful are autobiographical, or pretend to be. That is, they have definite rhetorical markers meant to make the reader think that he is attending to the poet's autobiography. And yet, at times it is impossible for Kees to have strict autobiography in mind—the "facts" simply do not jibe. One is left, therefore, with the paradox that these poems are fictive autobiographies, fictions pretending to be autobiographies. But the greatest majority of the remaining poems carry the standard Kees trademark. To some greater or lesser degree, they represent an effort by Kees to work in the surrealistic/expressionistic mode. As with the "autobiographical" poems, they differ in the degree to which they succeed.

Perhaps several of the poems appear to be autobiographical simply because we know something of the poet's life. "Problems of a Journalist" is primarily spoken in the voice of the poet-satirist, but our knowledge that Kees was a literary journalist, forced to work for *Time* and write newsreel scripts in order to make a living, suggests he is writing out of his own experience. The subject is clear enough to anyone old enough to remember all the agonizing of the 1940s and 1950s over those writers who had "sold out"—either to Hollywood or, in this case, to *Time* and other mass-circulation journals. Kees is satirizing those who say they want to get out but never leave: " 'I want to get away somewhere and re-read Proust,' / Said an editor of *Fortune* to a man on *Time.*" But, of course, he cannot get away, although Kees does not supply us with the usual economic reasons which make such departures difficult. Instead, he tells us in a beautifully apt image that the man cannot get away because the roads leading to the country and escape "fray like shawls / Outside the dusk of suburbs." The intensity with which Kees must have viewed this bondage induces the worst slip of taste in all his poetry. However damaging to pride and morale work-

ing for the Luce magazines was, it still could not be as bad as
the concentration camps and gulags. Yet that is what Kees compares it to: "Dachaus with telephones; Siberias with bonuses."
And the tasteless hyperbole of the line is simply reinforced by
Kees's description of the actual alternative to escape: "One
reads, as winter settles on the town, / The evening paper, in
an Irving Place café."

"Land's End" is another poem that might not be autobiographical at all, and yet one detail suggests that it is. The poem
is easy enough to understand. Using imagery of the area where
the sea meets the land, it switches from past to present tense
to describe a former hopeful experience and the present, more
pessimistic experience of the moment. But the speaker is very
specific about the amount of time that has passed: "Here where
I built my life ten years ago, / The day breaks gray and
cold. . . ." Perhaps the "I" is fictitious and so perhaps is the
length of time. But both elements seem to throw it back into
the personal.

"Return of the Ghost" could just as easily be completely
fictional, but a reader finding it in the *Collected Poems* is probably
more inclined to emphasize its personal quality simply because
it precedes two more patently autobiographical pieces, both of
which, like "Return of the Ghost," are based on a sense of
place. The ghost in question seems to be more of a spirit of
the place than anything else, and the speaker, remembering
the ghost from childhood, is trying to resurrect it. In other
words, he is trying to call up old associations, old memories
associated with the house. But, as is usual with Kees's work,
the speaker cannot be sure that bringing back the past is such
a terrific idea. Who but the ghost, he asks, "can prod us toward /
The past, our ruinous nostalgias?" Dwelling on the past may
be ruinous, but it is still the thing desired, and there is no
thought of not calling the ghost.

The next poem, "1926," suggests that the ghost did indeed
return, did indeed stir up memories. The poem is an extraordinarily economical and yet poignant foray into the past. It begins
with an evocation of the past in terms of specific images:

> The porchlight coming on again,
> Early November, the dead leaves

> Raked in piles, the wicker swing
> Creaking. Across the lots
> A phonograph is playing *Ja-Da*.

Every element is working here. The porchlight sets the right
"homey" atmosphere for the recollections of a boyhood in the
Midwest, the reference to November and dead leaves evokes
the right kind of autumnal longing, and the wicker swing both
reinforces our idea of a comfortable middle-class home and helps
place it in the past. What the speaker remembers is not just
the past of 1926, but the more immediate past in which some
of his former neighbors would suffer greatly. Some, by implication, would be wounded or killed in the war, one would go
insane, another would wind up fifteen years later with his throat
cut in Omaha.

But then Kees switches back to the year of the title, admitting
that he did not even know these unfortunates in 1926. Instead,
he remembers his airedale, scratching at the door as he returns
"from seeing Milton Sills / and Doris Kenyon. Twelve years
old."

Despite Kees's phrase in the previous poem, one is hard-
pressed to call this nostalgia "ruinous," but it is certainly painful,
and no more so than in its obvious juxtaposition of the daily
images and activities of a twelve-year old in Nebraska in 1926
and all the horrors that were to follow.

The next poem, "The Upstairs Room," suggests some of the
horrors followed soon after, though, in fact, the poem cannot
be entirely accurate as autobiography. Instead of the early November of "1926," this poem recalls an event in March of an
undetermined year. It does so while celebrating the lives of
four generations in terms of the wearing out of a carpet. The
carpet covers boards nailed in place by the speaker's "father's
father." Those boards are the floor "my father stained, / The
new blood streaming from his head." An allusion to a specific
gun's "Magnanimous and brutal smoke" later on leaves no
doubt that the father's suicide is being described. In fact Kees's
father survived the poet, so that the item can have no factual
basis. But the lack of factuality is more than made up in the
fictive power of the poem, and in the last lines the speaker
observes that it is now August and the floor is not stained but

"blank, worn smooth" and locked so firmly in his memory that it is "imperishable."

A Note of Humor

Alongside the items which, read autobiographically, suggest that Kees was nearing the end of his tether are some poems in which he attempts a more humorous or sardonic view of the world. They do not always succeed, for he cannot leave doomsday behind, but the humorous intent is certainly there. In "Wet Thursday," the narrator is visited on a thoroughly miserable evening by the oldest, most primeval cat he has ever seen. The cat proposes to live out his nine lives with the speaker, to be his "spiteful and envenomed shadow." But, surrounded by terrible weather, the cat goes promptly to sleep, "like an old campaigner." At least part of creation, Kees seems to be saying, is untouched by angst or any sense of dread.

"Weather for Pilgrims" is another attempt at a gayer vision, again only partly successful. The poem seems a poetic capturing of the energy and delight of a family occasion, much as it might be portrayed on canvas by Marc Chagall. Thanksgiving is what is being celebrated, with the usual assortment of drunken uncles, plump, stuffed turkeys, and, for good measure, the old Chevrolet breaking down on the way home.

The Horrific Once More

Of Kees's more-or-less horrific efforts, the ones least satisfying are those in which the grand-guignol effects seem to come off almost without thought and with very little defensible intention. "La Vita Nouva," for instance, is a fourteen-line poem addressed to the speaker's lover and built around the speaker's assumption of the body of a legless beggar. The speaker has actually witnessed such a beggar during the summer; now he lurches towards his beloved on calloused hands in the "losing" autumn. Why things are so desperate is never made clear; consequently, the grotesqueness seems to operate simply for the sake of perversity.

That same sense of perversity informs "The Coming of the Plague." Naturalistic function has been left completely behind in favor of what might be called the pathetic fallacy of the grotesque. In other words, no real or recognizable place is being described; instead, all of nature is shown to be acting in an unnatural and terrifying way. Obviously something is wrong with the universe, but in the absence of some explanation or cause, one simply comes away feeling the whole thing is one of Kees's finger exercises.

And certainly, as his whole career proves, Kees was good at such exercises. But in some he is capable of toning down the horror and increasing the inventiveness at the same time. For example, "The Base" is about the end of the world, but unlike "The Coming of the Plague" shows a real ingenuity in describing such an apocalypse. The poem is built around the paradox that everything *appears* to be verdant and fecund, but it is all a mirage. For the whole cosmos has been poisoned, and the signs are scarely hidden: "We scaled / The tallest pine and found it rotting at the top." Down below someone has sealed the veins of the leaves and "faked" the color. The poem ends with the mirage intact, at least for most. "And here we build, and gather, and are fed." The speaker never intimates that others are aware of his apocalyptic vision, and the ending is perhaps ambiguous on that account. But whether they are serenely awaiting the end or are for the most part unaware of its imminence, the poem is equally eerie.

In two other poems, "Darkness" and "January," the horrors are both toned down—though certainly not done away with—and the emphasis is more on the mind of the speaker. That is, there is no attempt to confuse his perception of the world with any objective, all-encompassing doom. In the first, he has a vision of a darkness that is going to overcome him just "as though one had pulled a string[,] / In an unfamiliar house, of a dim light. . . ." In "January," the speaker equates his death wish to the outside season, concluding that "Sleep is too short a death." But the correlations between the cold, dead season and the speaker's perceptions remain just that, and hence make the poem psychologically convincing as the account of the perceptions of a solitary consciousness.

The "I" becomes more self-conscious in "Farrago"—a poem that starts out with a set of bizarre descriptions which puzzle but give off certain hints of fertility rituals. But then the "I" breaks in and admits that it is all fictive. He is really sitting in a bar "On Tenth Street, writing down these lines / In the worst winter of my life." Having made his confession, the sense of futility overcomes him once again, and the bizarre imagery with which he opened the poem now closes it. It is too much of a burden to make sense out of the world. In at least one poem the "I" is obviously the restricted consciousness of the poem, although this "I" is not even human. Instead, the speaker in "Dog" is a canine. But he is beset with much the same problem as the "I" in "Farrago"—the world outside is overwhelmingly oppressive. So much so, in fact, that he loses his identity and his memory. Unable to remember his name—or even his breed—he "pant[s] at every door tonight." But rather than retreating into a death wish, he decides to throw himself into the flux:

> I can at least run howling toward the bankrupt lights
> Into the traffic where bones, cats, and masters swarm.
> And where my name must be.

The same level of inventiveness combined with horrific effects and an obviously fictional narrator is found in "Saratoga Ending," one of Kees's more impressive poems in the whole volume. This time, however, the narrator is human. The title probably refers to Saratoga Springs, famous both as a race track and as a health resort, where fashionable people come to "take the waters." But Kees has turned it, through his use of detail and imagery, into an international resort for the grotesque. Besides the paralysed patients, the pain-wracked and opium-addicted European aristocrats, Kees adds details that make one think of a Catholic shrine such as Lourdes. But if there are crutches and canes lined up on the wall, no miracles seem to be working at the moment.

The last stanza is a magnificent mixture of the diurnal and the apocalyptic as sounds and images produce the most ambiguous reactions in the speaker's mind. He hears glasses rattling—in reality the paraphernalia on the medicine cart outside his room—and it sounds just like "glasses being removed after / A party is over and the guests have gone." He touches a tongue depressor he uses for a bookmark and suddenly the warmth of the wood transports him many years backward to a spot where he was much happier and to a face:

Of one long dead who, high above the shore,
Looked down on waves across the sand, on rows of yellow jars
In which the lemon trees were ripening.

While the image of lemon trees ripening in jars is somewhat obscure, the image is obviously one of a happy youth, and the mood is one of joyous recollection. Thus this poem joins the very few in the Kees canon where he is willing to admit the possibility of the past not being ruinous but in some ways a joyful contrast to the present.

But Kees's more mordant self usually prevails, even when he is trying for a little whimsy. Thus, in "Colloquy," another of the poems about animals in this volume, the speaker brings a plate of liver to a cat in order to ask the cat about the human condition. The speaker, of course, already knows that the world is in bad shape, but he wants to know "Where / Are we now? Do we know anything?" The cat's only reply is "Give me the dish." But the speaker gets the cat's meaning. "I had his answer," he observes in the last line, "wise as yours."

And if cats know nothing about humanity, nature herself is indifferent at best. "The Beach in August" is Kees's meditation on the nature of mortality, and the most striking item in the poem is his view of nature's indifference. A woman walks into the sea and drowns, and the tide brings in old fruit. The human condition—a phrase Kees uses twice in the poem—is to

> . . . dry and lie in the sun
> While the seascape arranges old fruit,
> Coming in with the tide, glistening
> At noon.

The lines contain the hint that nature is something of the detached modern artist, just as the cat is something of a cynical savant.

A Short Prayer

Kees himself could be both artist, cynic, and savant on occasion. But, for the most part, he seemed to consider himself just another piece of suffering humanity. Thus it is fitting that the last poem in the volume is a "Small Prayer" from a tortured soul, not an artist or thinker. It is short and intense, so intense that it deserves favorable comparison with Gerard Manley Hopkins's famous "terrible" sonnets and also deserves to be quoted in full:

> Change, move, dead clock, that this fresh day
> May break with dazzling light to these sick eyes.
> Burn, glare, old sun, so long unseen,
> That time may find its sound again, and cleanse
> What ever it is that a wound remembers
> After the healing ends.

Chapter Six

Uncollected Poems and "The Waiting Room"

Recognizable Merit

At the end of each edition of the *Collected Poems,* Donald Justice has included a number of poems that Kees either wrote after *Poems 1947–1954* went to press or that he chose not to publish in any of his first three volumes. In the revised edition, Justice prints fifteen poems, arranged in what, on the basis of available evidence, would seem to be their order of composition.[1]

Almost all of the poems have recognizable merit; at least one seems to rank with the best of Kees's canon. In some cases it is easy to speculate as to why Kees chose not to reprint a particular poem in book form; in others such hypothesizing is more difficult. Most surprisingly, perhaps, the poems would seem to form an almost perfect microcosm of Kees's total oeuvre. Almost every voice, every technique, every theme explored in his three published volumes is represented here.

The earliest poem, for example, reminds one of the rare, quiet, reflective tone found so rarely in Kees, reminds one in fact of the very atypical "Praise to the Mind" of his first volume. "To Build a Quiet City in His Mind" is a simply stated wish to have some inner refuge against the onslaughts of the mad, external world, a wish the speaker refuses to give up:

> Yet in spite of loss and guilt
> And hurricanes of time, it might be built:
>
> A refuge, permanent, with trees that shade
> When all the other cities die and fade.

Perhaps in abandoning this poem, Kees also abandoned the wish.

Other poems were quite possibly abandoned because more successful poems of the same sort were available. "To a Noisy Contemporary" is far more Juvenalian, far less subtle than the similarly named "To A Contemporary." As invective, however, it certainly must be said to get its point across. Addressed to a totally egotistical author, Kees sums up his work succinctly: "As an entertainment, zero." And his not-too-subtle parting line lets one know what Kees thinks of the author's subtlety: "You may well supplant the tuba if the music lasts."

"The Older Programs That We Falsified" is an attack aimed a little wider. This time it is not an individual but a group that bears the brunt of the author's satire. Kees has chosen to disparage the politically doctrinaire mind before; this time it is done with even more vitriol. He reminds them that they are getting older and that their ranks are thinning. Some of their comrades have defected, some discovered that their outrage was really not social but psychological in origin—and hence have turned to psychiatrists instead of the party for help—and some have simply "shot themselves in bathrooms." But the faithful remain, reunited ten years later, and for all that has happened and all the falsification that has taken place, seemingly no wiser for it. The poem seems to be an attack on the Stalinist mind that only a postwar sensibility could conjure up, but in tone it is not much different from Kees's earlier attacks on turncoat-pacifists.

Postwar sensibility is also responsible for Kees's doomsday poems, of course; and, sure enough, there is a poem about the end of civilization among this handful of uncollected efforts. "The End of the Library" records what happened to the instruments of culture "When the coal / Gave out. . . ." What is amazing about this little piece of science fiction is the incredibly understated tone the speaker uses in describing how the burning of the contents of the library managed to keep them warm:

> First the set
> Of Bulwer-Lytton
> And then the Walter Scott.
> They gave a lot of warmth.
> Toward the end, in
> February, flames

> Consumed the Greek
> Tragedians and Baudelaire,
> Proust, Robert Burton
> And the Po-Chu-i. Ice
> Thickened on the sills.
> More for the sake of the cat,
> We said, than for ourselves,
> Who huddled, shivering,
> Against the stove
> All winter long.

It is a final, devastating irony, of course, that the books are being burned more for the sake of a cat than for the humans. It is an irony which the speaker does not see, however, anymore than he hears his "objective" assessment of the relative warmth each author gives. Civilization is literally being burned up in front of him, but the disaster that brought it and the speaker to this predicament has obviously also separated the speaker from any real sense of the loss that is taking place.

But doomsday is not the only direction of Kees's fantasy in these poems. There is also "The Bunyip," a poem about a mythical beast "about the size / Of a full-grown calf." The poem reminds one of "The Umbrella" in *Poems 1947–1954,* the only difference being that it has less scope and deals with an object for whom one can develop sympathy. Thus it is not only the charm of the myths themselves that attract us. We are also moved by the plight of the bunyip, "Crying sometimes, after dark, that it is not / Extinct, imaginary, or a myth. . . ."

Kees feels much more free to create his mythical animal than he does to imagine what ordinary cats must do during the day, while their owners are away. All of "The Cats," in fact, is devoted to professing his ignorance on the subject. "It is a dull neighborhood," he admits, with the only excitement coming from the sounds of the playground and the cars whizzing by "in a bluish light." At six o'clock the cats are there "When we come home from work / To greet us," but what they do during the day remains a mystery. "The Cats" is the last poem in the book, suggesting that Kees must have written it during the last two years of his life. Whatever torments or depressions he must have been suffering are kept completely out of this poem.

But the penultimate poem is another story. Entitled "A Musician's Wife," it is a plaintive monologue uttered by the wife
of a once brilliant, now insane pianist. Unlike so many of Kees's
poems, this one shows no awareness of the world at large—or
at least makes very little effort to blame that world for the
pianist's misfortunes. Instead, the wife is quietly resigned to
her own misfortune and quietly wrapped up in her routine of
living with a sister nearby the sanitarium and visiting a husband
who does not even return her gaze. The first half of the five-
stanza poem is given over to a description of her husband—a
description entirely devoid of self-pity:

> Between the visits to the shock ward
> The doctors used to let you play
> On the old upright Baldwin . . . .
>
> And all day long you played Chopin,
> Badly and hauntingly, when you weren't
> Screaming on the porch that looked
> Like an enormous birdcage.

But in her understated way, she does not so much hide her
sorrow as reveal it. Always, as she tells us, when she has returned
from her futile visit, she gets out his marvelous recordings "that
nobody bought" and plays them. But it is not the music of
those worn-out recordings that disturbs her most:

> Now, sometimes, I wake in the night
> And hear the sound of dead leaves
> Against the shutters. And then a distant
> Music starts, a music out of an abyss,
> And it is dawn before I sleep again.

If the theme of mental illness is not unusual for Kees, surely
the loyalty of the speaker for her husband, free of any self-
pity or accusation, is extremely rare.

And there is yet another poem that embraces the possibilities
of love or affection: "Late Evening Song." The poem is, once
again, a monologue, with the speaker indicating that, against
all expectation, he is capable of feeling some affection for his
companion:

> For a while
> Let it be enough:
> The responsive smile,
> Though effort goes into it.

The effort, of course, does not indicate any disapproval of the companion, but a reluctance, in view of past experiences, to enter any kind of relationship. Nevertheless, the smile is there and the poem ends by reacknowledging its presence. Perhaps for the moment it can only be formed in the softer light of night and with the memory of the fires that quenched it earlier. But nevertheless, the speaker admits, "I look at you / Across those fires and the dark."

The renewal of the possibility of love is matched in "Covering Two Years" by a renewal of personality, a return from a psychological void. The poem begins with a series of metaphors for the "nothingness that feeds upon itself"—that is, for the loss of personal identity that the speaker has been suffering for the last two years. Each of the metaphors seems perfect for the job at hand:

> Pencils that turn to water in the hand,
> Parts of a sentence, hanging in the air,
> Thoughts breaking in the mind like glass,
> Blank sheets of paper that reflect the world
> Whitened the world that I was silenced by.

The poem makes no attempt to describe the process of restoration or to go into what psychic shock caused this extreme loss of orientation. Instead the speaker simply intimates that time has ameliorated the problems until the speaker can suddenly reorient himself and experience once again—not thoughts breaking in the mind like glass—but the making of connections, the rediscovered "knowledge of recurrence and return."

The return of self is both cause for celebration and a mixed blessing—not all of the recurrent memories are consolatory. "That Figure With the Moulting Beard" is about a figure from the past who keeps reappearing in the present. Superficially, the poem resembles "Relating to Robinson," the poem in which Robinson is described by the speaker as an almost spectral figure

who haunts the streets of New York. But here Kees's aim is
more universal:

> That figure with the moulting beard and ancient stare
> You thought you had escaped in Brooklyn Heights
> You'll reckon with again, pursuing you down 63rd Street,
> Yet quite unhurried, almost sanguine, one might say.

The moult and the "ancient stare" begin to give the point away,
of course. This is no ordinary pursuer; this is an archetype of
Death. So, the poem goes on, "you" will see him again two
years later in Los Angeles, and again there will be no pursuit.
But sometimes, of course, "Here perhaps, perhaps in Wichita,"
there will be a "last time." And if the place is uncertain, other
things are less so:

> But of the lead pipe in his pocket and the knife,
> The torch, the poison, and the nails, no doubt at all.

The series of instruments of death starts masterfully with a fairly
up-to-date one and ends with a reminder that even a god-figure
could not escape the fate of all. Needless to say, the poem is
even more horrific because the only death seemingly contem-
plated is a violent one.

Another Masterpiece

Many of the uncollected poems, then, have merit. But there
is one poem, "Place of Execution," that goes far beyond mere
merit. Like many of Kees's best poems, it is somewhat longer
than most: in this case, sixty-six lines. And also as in many of
Kees's best poems, the lines of influence are clearly visible,
or rather clearly heard. There is much here of the reflective
Eliot and Auden, and it is all used to good advantage. It is
also an incredible combination of the poetry of direct statement
and the poetry of symbolic and imagistic indirection. And it is
finally a poem that somehow manages to maintain an elegant,
lucid, balanced tone in the face of an extremely forlorn topic
and conclusion.

The theme of the poem is commonplace enough: the displace-

ment of childhood illusions by the pressures of maturity. "Where
are the marvelous cities that our childhoods built for us," the
speaker begins the poem by asking. And in a number of equally
relaxed lines he goes on to describe how beautiful those "cities"
and landscapes and seascapes were. Now nothing remains of
the "golden beaches" and "green fields" of our youth; and:

> If we walk along the empty foreground of the sea,
> The wind is cold, and there is only darkness
>   at our backs.

The second part of the poem retraces the import of the first
in another set of images. The world is not only distorted through
the eyes of childhood, but when seen through a goldfish bowl
as well. But even goldfish perceive some of the real world—
doors slamming, constant quarrels, etc. And, of course, the glass
bowl is always vulnerable, and can even become, in the phrase
of the title, a place of execution:

> And one day someone broke the goldfish bowl,
>   or it fell;
> Anyway, the fish were dead on the floor, among
>   the broken glass.

And now the goldfish, both illusioned and disillusioned, will
take their place among the recurring images of the poem.

The third part of the poem begins with a hypothetical question
that goes nowhere. "If you walk among the foreground of the
sea," the questioner begins, and observe all the usual
sights. . . . But then he breaks off to ask an even more frightening question: "What if there is no sea?" This question will not
do either; it is time to acknowledge mundane reality and stop
inventing melodramatic situations. It is more probable, he admits, that "you" are leading your normal, routine, boring, frus-
trating life, perhaps in a "middle-class slum." And the
unspectacular day will end in darkness, until the street lights
turn on. Then, in a passage which seems to combine the proph-
etic voice of Eliot with the more urbane and up-to-date vocabu-
lary of Auden, the speaker describes where we have wound
up:

We have arrived, finally, at the celebration
Where there is nothing to celebrate.
In a landscape of dubious interest
With odors of unaired rooms and the less pleasant aroma
Of last year's socio-economic predictions.
An erubescent Santa Claus grins from a window,
Sawdust running out of his side.

The blushing Santa Claus behind the glass is supposed to remind
us of the earlier goldfish in their bowl, I suspect, just as the
unaired rooms play off the perfect rooms in perfect houses we
imagined in childhood. Kees can have both his poetry of statement and his symbolic progression in the same passage.

And it must be admitted that symbolic progression or symbolic
recurrence is just about all that follows in the final part of the
poem. There is no redemption in this poem, no return to childhood, so there can be no genuine movement. But there is a
magnificent bringing together of all the images of the poem
for one last appearance, beginning with the image of the city
once again. But this city is the grown-up city, the city we greet
every morning as it emerges from the dreary fog, the city of
"rusty grillwork and the nailed-up doors," of "dirty snow" and
"mournful cats." Playing on the image of the dirty snow, the
speaker concludes, "The day takes on the color of the street."

These images are followed by another series detailing "What
we have come to know," but this time the catalog lacks any
verve, opting instead to rehearse the dreary clichés of reality:
"false predictions, shattered promises," "vacant and relentless
dawns." And finally Kees tries to make the poem come full
circle by reminding us of the fate of the goldfish ("The bowl
breaks and the fish gasp on the floor."), and then returning
to the cities and noting how now they are not being built by
childhood, but, "in distances of waste" they "are unbuilt."
"Place of Execution" is a splendid example of how poetry can
turn a trite observation into a deeply felt experience.

"The Waiting Room"

Although Kees is known to have written some dramas in
his undergraduate years, "The Waiting Room" would seem

to be his only mature work in that genre.[2] The play was probably composed—or at least was still being worked on—after 1952, since one of the characters reads a fragment of a headline ("Ike Foresees Prosperous Future For. . . .") which sounds more like the presidential than the military Eisenhower. It was never completely finished. But it has been noted and praised by Kenneth Rexroth[3] and deserves serious attention. Because of its unavailability, the following analysis will be more exhaustive than usual.

Everything we have examined of Kees so far suggests that he was a man who worked within established conventions rather than creating new ones. The short fiction was obviously indebted to several of the predominant modes of fiction writing available at the time: regional satire, economic determinism, and, at least on one occasion, bittersweet Hemingway. The poetry, of course, was heavily indebted to men whom we still think of as the modern masters—Eliot and Auden—and to certain influences— symbolism, expressionism, surrealism—easier to name as movements than to associate with individual poets. Much the same is true of Kees as dramatist: he absorbs and reworks several strains of the current dramatic tradition rather than embarking on anything totally original. Doubtless it was this talent to draw on many examples around him, while—at least in the poetry— making the tradition his own, that also allowed him to become an accomplished painter, musician, photographer, and filmmaker in such a compressed period of time.

What is interesting about the question of influence on Kees's mature drama is that his source has changed once again. In *The Last Man,* "A Cornucopia for Daily Use" showed that he could imitate Eliot's minor dramatic style—the style of several dramatic fragments such as "Sweeney Agonistes." But there is no hint of that sardonic and slightly absurd use of the banal dialogue of daily life in "The Waiting Room." Nor does he go to either Eliot or Auden for direction in how to write a genuine verse drama. Eliot's experiments in *Murder in the Cathedral* and Auden's in *For the Time Being,* for example, would seem to have no interest for Kees.

Instead, he has written a drama about three women (Jill, Patrecia [*sic*], and Nancy) engaged in the process of self-discovery. They meet, by chance apparently, in a "waiting room," talk about their psychological hangups, react against one another's problems and probings; and then two of the three leave, believing, in effect, that they have found their own cure. Their language seems totally naturalistic:

Jill: We came in the door and all the lights were out and Phillip said, "Oh, my God you've left the oven on again." As if *he* never made a mistake in his life. What about the time he got the case of Scotch from a client of his in the South and left it out there in the hallway? I *always* thought those two boys who lived across the hall are the ones who stole it. Twelve quarts of Dewar's White Label. . . . "Oh my God you've left the oven on," he said. As if. . . .

Kees, of course, had many "voices" in his poetry, many meant to suggest a fictional persona. But the voice above seems to be completely different. Here there is no striving after poetic effect, no movement toward the neatly turned line, the encapsulating statement that gets its power from the tension between passion and the formal constraint of verse. Nor is this dialogue at all like that of his short stories—if for no other reason than that it is not at all condescending. Instead, the sympathy is clearly with the speaker. Her psychological dilemma is properly respected, and there are no tricks meant to force the reader to look down his nose at her.

Naturalism itself is a convention. Here the rhythms may be akin to the "natural" rhythms of prose, but the context is redolent with the conventions of twentieth-century drama. The dialogue is obviously a public probing of a private psychological wound, a probing that is taking place in front of two strangers with only the slightest of provocations. Psyches tend to confront themselves and one another more readily, more artificially, and with more articulation on stage than they do in real life.

This probing of the psyche along with its concomitant aim of allowing the characters eventually to take charge of their own destinies suggest what Kees's major thematic influence in this work might very well be. Jean-Paul Sartre's *No Exit* was published in Stuart Gilbert's English translation in 1947. At least by the early 1950s, Sartre had become almost a household word, and existentialism had become the philosophy most in vogue. *No Exit* certainly has a more ornate setting ("A drawing room in the Second Empire style") and far more pessimistic conclusion, since the drawing room is part of hell and the characters are drawn to discover that "hell is other people." The play ends, in fact, with the three main characters—two women and a man—looking forward to an eternity of tormenting one another. But along the way, as the horrible truth is dawning on them, they spend much time going over their own lives, alternately rationalizing their shortcomings, their lack of authenticity, and facing up to the uncomfortable truth. The dialogue reads, at least in Gilbert's translation, much like Kees; and though Sartre's play is at least twice as long, there is the same absence of real action, the same movement between reverie and interaction on the part of the characters. Certainly *No Exit* is closer to "The Waiting Room" than anything by Kees's former masters is, just as Kees's play is doubtless more "existential" than anything else in his oeuvre. But before discussing thematics, perhaps it would be wise to examine the state of the manuscript and the state of the playwright's technical expertise.

Text and Technique

It is possible that the manuscript was edited after Kees's death by his father, John Kees, who did indeed try to gather his son's literary remains together. At the very least John Kees added a cover sheet, on the back of which he typed the following inscription:

Copyright 1961 by The Estate of Weldon Kees,
John Kees, Trustee.
2457 South 27th. [*sic*] Street, Lincoln Nebraska
Manufactured in the United States of America

The typeface is the same style used to type the rest of the manuscript, but there are enough crossouts and misspellings in the text to suggest that it is Weldon's less-than-finished copy rather than John's attempt at a fair copy of his son's work.

Nevertheless, the play is certainly in final enough shape to be performed. It is sixteen pages long, double-spaced with very narrow margins. It would probably take approximately thirty minutes to stage. And, perhaps not surprisingly for someone

like Kees who seemed to specialize in excelling in all disciplines,
it shows a remarkable grasp of stage conventions and a remarkable use of stage machinery. Note Kees's initial stage directions:

(A bare stage, except for a long bench of the kind used in bus and
railroad stations. Lights up slowly: harsh intense day. Seated on the
bench are Jill and Patrecia. Jill is looking through a newspaper: Patrecia
has a magazine in her lap. Jill looks curiously at Patrecia; goes back
to her paper. Patrecia looks curiously at Jill as Nancy enters; P smiles
at N, then picks up magazine and goes through it idly, bored. Nancy
carries a book and a balloon on a stick. She takes a handkerchief
from her pocketbook; she is on the verge of tears. Glances to see if
the other two are looking at her; dabs at her eyes, blows her nose.
Patrecia looks at the balloon.)

Obviously Kees is very much aware of the conventions of
stage acting and of the iconography of stage settings. The actors
are immediately set in motion, catching the audience's attention,
forcing the audience to begin to make tentative judgments of
their personalities, and also beginning to interact with one another, setting up the conflicts that should propel the drama.

The bareness of the stage setting suggests the kind of avant-garde minimal set that Kees was doubtless familiar with; Kees
is not simply adapting a fashionable convention. A single bench
on a bare stage, without any indication that a specific bus or
train station or other waiting room with a socially functional
purpose is being evoked, leads the audience to assume that
the play is taking place within a metaphoric setting. Kees's "waiting room" is certainly that. And the harsh lighting underlines
not only the metaphoric nature of the setting but also insists
that the action taking place, in effect, will be bitter medicine:
no easy wish-fulfillments will be offered during this performance.
The audience is readied to see characters suffer and undergo
some painful experiences. (Bringing the lights up slowly simply
lets the audience have its suspense—are we to have a harshly
lit metaphoric setting?—and then the satisfaction of having its
suspicions confirmed.) In short, Kees's "bare minimum" is purposeful and not simply fashionable or simple minded.

Throughout the play, in fact, Kees calls on the technical resources of the theatre to carry the drama. Characters appear and disappear by means of spotlighting rather than making conventional entrances. Colored spotlights are used to introduce characters who figure only in the reveries of the principals, with different colors for different characters. Music is used to evoke a mood of the past, such as Patrecia's memories of her ballet lessons as a little girl. To say the least, Kees very obviously did not intend this to be a mere closet drama.

The Action

The play opens with Nancy explaining why she is carrying the balloon. "I got it for my little boy. He and his father are meeting me here." Then Jill ("as though to herself": Kees is careful not to get them too involved too quickly) begins to read from the newspaper's advice-to-the-lovelorn column. The letter she reads allows Kees the satirist to comment sardonically on the banality of existence, but it is also thematically important, since the writer of the letter is a woman having problems with her lover. Each of the three women will shortly reveal her own problems with a male figure; indeed, each is apparently waiting on a man—although it is never really made clear that they are. Then Kees reinforces the symbolical nature of the play by having the characters ask one another for the time. Of course, no one has the time, although, significantly, Nancy has a broken watch. The characters will be more or less frozen in time until they sort out their difficulties, will be left in the waiting room until they can find authentic and integrated selves.

After the exchange about "time," Jill slips rather easily into a recollection (still "to herself") about a painful moment in her past when she left the oven on in her apartment and the escaping gas killed her parakeets. What is really painful about the memory is the guilt feelings reinforced by the man she was living with—but she is not ready to mention that yet. Then after Patrecia reads some silliness from a fashion magazine (which does not do much to establish her position in the play), Nancy breaks the ice by reading a sonnet about "unended love" from Edna St. Vincent Millay—a type of love she has never had.

While they are waiting, each manages to reveal her own difficulties: Patrecia and Nancy are visited by apparitions from the

past, and Nancy is visited by "a man with a cigar" who appears
out of nowhere, pesters her, and is finally driven off by Patrecia.
His significance is never made clear.

Patrecia is actually the first to reveal her past. She is a former
actress, it turns out, one whose mother put her in ballet slippers
"the minute I was able to stand without holding on to something": "Dear old mother, my foot. She was one of those real
shoving, pushing, ruthless, ambitious women that missed the
boat and want to get their daughters on another one."

She has more ambivalent feelings, as she will reveal later in
the drama, about her former lover, a theatrical agent named
Shackelton. Kees's introduction to Shackelton and his use of
him shows how he is about to sprinkle humor throughout the
proceedings:

I started to tell you about this man, Bert Shackelton (*Spot on Shackelton
sitting at his desk with feet up, reading* Variety). Well, he turned out
to be one of the most unusual men in the world—an honest agent.
(*Shackelton assumes an expression of absolute rectitude.*) Well, honest most
of the time (*Shackelton looks as though he is scheming up something*).

Patrecia's real problem is that she was in love with Shackelton,
a married man. Later in the drama, after she has been affected
by the other women so that her voice is "very husky," her
"brassiness . . . all gone," she relives a traumatic moment in
a hotel room when she had the opportunity to seduce and perhaps gain permanent possession of him. But she could not bring
herself to do it:

I remember an electric fan whining and that terrible wall-paper with
roses. . . . I knew what I wanted . . . I knew just what to do. . . .
I could have done it and in no time we'd have been (*Long pause*) I
couldn't do it. I couldn't do it to him.

What causes her failure is not clear. She has just been lamenting
that Bert was *happily* married and always looked at her as if
she were a "thing." Her choice of words probably means he
simply looked at her as a client rather than a lover. Whatever,
it is this destructive past that Patrecia must overcome.

Jill, the oldest and most promiscuous of the three, functions most clearly as the one who must comment on the general state that exists between the sexes. She is bitter about all the men in her life, bitter about the way they treat women, bitter about the gross and hypocritical ways they behave. But she also has to come to terms with her defects:

. . . Love: I got to the point where I was in *love* with jealousy. I don't even know why. I was wild with it. I was playing two men against each other for everything I could. It would be late, late at night. . . . I was living in New York. One would call me up . . . the phone would ring . . . and I'd be in bed with the other one . . . I could feel his jealosy on the back of my neck and the other one's jealosy coming over the phone like a red-hot wire. I didn't even think of it as jealosy, I just thought . . . me . . . me[.]

After this speech, Jill has stopped blaming all on others, has come to terms with her self, and is free to take charge of her existence, which she will shortly do.

Nancy is both the youngest and the most disturbed of the three. And her problems seem to be all Oedipal. She suffers from delusions, so that she thinks the older Jill is her mother; and a great deal of the emotional impact of the play comes from the manic scenes in which Nancy, caught up in the delusion and in the painful but intense re-creation of her past, manhandles Jill and assaults her with all the pent-up rage a daughter can have for a detested mother. Nancy's father is dead, a suicide whose end was brought on by his wife (according to Nancy). In fact, the portrait of the mother is quite conventional, especially when one considers that the play was written at a time when "Momism" was an extremely popular topic. American mothers were seen as social-climbing, superprotective, super-squeamish sorts who tried to mold their children into rigid imitations of themselves and wound up visiting mental illness upon their offspring. And Nancy's mother, like most of the stereotypes, never concedes responsibility or even that her daughter is sick. (One of the things Nancy holds against her is that she refused to allow Nancy to have shock treatment.) Sometimes Nancy is almost too articulate in her self-analysis:

(*Trying hard to think*) It's . . . not . . . right growing up. I go back over it all the time and try to. . . . (*She stands up and walks rigidly, semi-catatonic; to Jill*) Don't pretend you're not my mother. Those are my mother's shoes. When I was a little girl . . . the ignominy, he said, the ignominy of growing up . . . growing up . . . growing up.

After this speech she steps into Jill's temporarily discarded shoes and slowly regresses in action and posture to a "girl of ten." The mother, incidentally, is the only apparition given her own lines. She certainly proves to be, in the language of the stage direction, "a real horror."

By the end of the play Nancy will have worked some of the pent-up energy out of her system but will come to no real solution of her mental crisis. On the other hand, both Jill and Patrecia will have their cathartic speeches and exhibit a newly found determination to leave the waiting room and take more direct control of their lives.

If its indebtedness to existentialism tends to date "The Waiting Room," its focus on feminine psychology makes it seem arrestingly contemporary. "The Waiting Room" deserves production and, more important, deserves to become part of Kees's published canon.

Chapter Seven

Future Prospects
for Weldon Kees

The twentieth century has produced many fine poets, but none who could write poetry as well as Weldon Kees and still find time to be an accomplished musician, painter, collagist, photographer, and filmmaker. One index of artistic success is the variety of critical studies and perspectives a career can sustain. In Kees's case the variety is impressive. Kees's thematic concerns merit study, for they are central even if unusually morbid. The major questions of the rationality of our culture and even of our mental structures are raised again and again by Kees. Kees also ought to be studied because of the excellent example his work affords of what happens to a tradition when it passes beyond its founders. Of late there has been much said about the "anxiety of influence"—that psychological phenomenon which forces truly major figures to break sharply with their poetic forebears—but little about the more normal process of influence where disciples more modestly adapt and expand what has been left to them. Kees, as a second-generation modernist, comfortable within the tradition, would be a good subject for such a study.

He should also be read and studied because of what we have called his "doomsday" poems—those poems obviously inspired by the birth of the atomic age. Kees had a sensibility ready to accept and brood on such frightening possibilities as the atomic age gave rise to—it is possible that no poet of his generation was more obsessed with the prospect of total annihilation. That sensibility was perhaps responsible for his suicide—a fate of many of the poets of his generation. The question obviously should not be the suicide itself but the unhappiness that so many—Berryman, Jarrell, Delmore Schwartz—seemed to carry with them. Was such unhappiness part and parcel of being a poet, or were they simply poets who also suffered from major psychological depressions?

Obviously the last sentence suggests the need for biographical studies, and there is one other interesting area that a proper critical biography could shed light on. No other figure in this century seems to have engaged successfully in as many artistic disciplines as Weldon Kees. A study of Kees's life would produce not only a literary biography but a fascinating account of the interrelationships among the arts. The very rapidity with which Kees moved from one form or medium to another suggests that he was able to transform the insights or some of the understanding of one medium into successful expression in another. But the mechanics of such transformation are simply not known. Kees's career could provide some answers in the psychology of creativity.

Of work currently underway on Kees, perhaps three projects are most significant. Professor John McKerman of Marshall University is currently engaged in writing a biography of Kees. Professor Robert E. Knoll, of the University of Nebraska, is editing Kees's letters for eventual publication, under the aegis of the Center for Great Plains Studies. In addition to telling us much about Kees, Professor Knoll feels that the letters will provide great insight into the cultural life of the poet's times. Finally, Dana Gioia, who helped edit the special edition devoted to Kees by the journal *Sequoia*, has published an edition of Kees's better short fiction, *The Ceremony and Other Stories*. Such interest and activity guarantee that Weldon Kees's unique and yet immensely relevant poetic voice will continue to be heard.

Notes and References

Chapter One

1. For much of the biographical information in this chapter, I am indebted to Professor William Zander of Fairleigh Dickinson University. Professor Zander generously shared research he had done on Kees while a graduate student at the University of Missouri. Professor Zander was able to interview Kees's mother several times before her death.
2. *The Collected Poems of Weldon Kees,* ed. Donald Justice (Iowa City, Iowa: 1960). Reissued in a Bison Book edition by the University of Nebraska Press (Lincoln, Nebr., 1962); revised edition issued in 1975.
3. "Weldon Kees: Solipsist as Poet," *Prairie Schooner* 35 (1961):33–41.
4. *New Republic,* 18 July 1955, 19.
5. *Nation,* 7 January 1950, 19.
6. *Nation,* 3 June 1950, 557.
7. "Robert Motherwell," *Magazine of Art,* March 1948, 86–88.
8. *Nation,* 1 October 1949, 327.
9. *New Republic,* 17 January 1955, 22.
10. *Partisan Review* 15 (1948):614–22. Reprinted in Chandler Brossard, ed., *The Scene Before You: A New Approach to American Culture* (New York: Dial Press, 1955), 230–38. References in the text are to the latter printing.
11. *New Republic,* 18 July 1955, 19.

Chapter Two

1. *Prairie Schooner* 8 (1934):179.
2. *Prairie Schooner* 11 (1937):310.
3. In Edward J. O'Brien, ed., *Best American Short Stories and the Yearbook of the American Short Story* (Boston:1941). Page references in the text.
4. *Prairie Schooner* 12 (1938). Page references in the text.
5. *Prairie Schooner* 10 (1936). Page references in the text.
6. *Frontier and Midland* 17 (1937). Page references in the text.

7. *Prairie Schooner* 13 (1939). Page references in the text.

8. *Hinterland*, n.s. 1, 3 (n.d.). Page references in the text.

9. *Hinterland*, n.s. 1, 2 (n.d.):33.

10. *New Directions in Prose and Poetry* (Norfolk, Conn.: New Directions, 1939). Page references in the text.

11. *Hinterland*, no. 10 (1938), 31.

12. *Little Man*, 4th ser. (1940), 14.

13. "Four Stories," *Rocky Mountain Review* 3, no.1 (1938):14.

14. *New Directions in Prose and Poetry* (Norfolk, Conn.: New Directions, 1940). Page references in text.

Chapter Three

1. All selections from *The Last Man* are cited as they appear in *The Collected Poems of Weldon Kees*, rev. ed., ed. Donald Justice (Lincoln: University of Nebraska Press, 1975), 1–44.

2. *The New Poetry: American and British Poetry Since World War II* (New York: Oxford University Press, 1967), 3–24.

3. Preface to *Collected Poems*, xix.

4. Ibid., xvi.

Chapter Four

1. Kees also included in *The Fall of Magicians* a poem called "Robinson," which proved to be the first of four poems involving a male denizen of a more-or-less horrific world. Since these poems are usually considered to be all of a piece and since the other three are included in *Poems 1947–1954*, "Robinson" will be considered along with them in the next chapter.

2. All selections from *The Fall of Magicians* are cited as they appear in *Collected Poems*, rev. ed., 45–84.

Chapter Five

1. All selections from *Poems 1947–1954* are cited as they appear in *Collected Poems*, rev. ed., 87–157.

2. For Dana Gioia's claim that Kees's view of Christ was influenced by his reading of Albert Schweitzer, see "The Achievement of Weldon Kees," *Sequoia* 37 (Spring 1979):37–38.

3. For a perceptive reading of the Robinson poems, see Sharon Mayer Libera, "The Disappearance of Weldon Kees," *Ploughshares* 5 (1979):155–158.

Chapter Six

1. Poems cited in this chapter are taken from "Uncollected Poems" in *Collected Poems,* rev. ed., 161–78.
2. I am indebted to Professor William Zander of Fairleigh Dickinson University for a photographic reproduction of a typescript of the play, a copy he obtained from Weldon Kees's mother in the early 1960s.
3. See Kenneth Rexroth, *Assays* (Norfolk, Conn.:1961), 236–37.

Selected Bibliography

PRIMARY SOURCES

1. *Poetry*
The Collected Poems of Weldon Kees. Edited by Donald Justice. Iowa City: Stone Wall Press, 1960. Reprint. Lincoln: University of Nebraska Press, 1962; rev. ed., 1975.
The Fall of Magicians. New York: Reynall & Hitchcock, 1947.
The Last Man. San Francisco: Colt Press, 1943.
Poems 1947–1954. San Francisco: Adrian Wilson, 1954.

2. *Short Stories*
"Applause." *Prairie Schooner* 13 (1937):128–31.
"The Ceremony." *Little Man,* 4th ser. (1940):8–14.
The Ceremony and Other Stories. Edited by Dana Gioia. Lincoln, Nebr.: Abattoir Editions, 1983.
"Downward and Away." *Hinterland,* no. 10 (1938), 31–36.
"Escape In Autumn." *Windsor Quarterly* 2 (1935):202–03.
"The Evening of the Fourth of July." In *New Directions in Prose and Poetry,* 56–72. Norfolk, Conn.: New Directions, 1940.
"Four Stories." *Rocky Mountain Review* 3, no. 1 (1938):7, 9–10.
"Gents 50¢; Ladies 25¢." *Hinterland,* n.s. 1 no. 3 [n.d.]: 31–34.
"I Should Worry." In *New Directions in Prose and Poetry,* 104–12. Norfolk, Conn.: New Directions, 1939.
"The Life of the Mind." In *Best American Short Stories and the Yearbook of the American Short Story: 1941.* Edited by Edward J. O'Brien, 161–73. Boston: Little, Brown & Co., 1941.
"A Man To Help." *Horizon,* January-February 1937, 9–12.
"Mrs. Lutz." *Prairie Schooner* 1 (1937):309–12.
"Saturday Rain." *Prairie Schooner* 8 (1934):179–83.
"So Cold Outside." *Prairie Schooner* 12 (1938):273–81.
"The Sign Painters." *Hinterland,* n.s. 2, no. 2 [n.d.]:31–34.
"This Is Home." *Manuscript,* May-June 1936, 30–33.
"Three Pretty Nifty Green Suits." *Prairie Schooner* 10 (1936):292–300.
"Three Young Priests." *Rocky Mountain Review* 5, no. 2 (1940):4–5.
"A Walk Home." *Frontier and Midland* 17 (1937):166–70.

3. *Criticism, Essays, and Reviews*
"American Taste and Whimsy." [Review of Russell Lynes's *The Taste-makers.*] *New Republic,* 17 January 1955, 21–22.
"Art." *Nation,* 7 January 1950, 18–19; 3 June 1950, 556–57.
"Dondero and Dada." *Nation,* 1 October 1949, 327.
"How To Be Happy: Installment 1053." [Review of Arnold Hutsch-neker's *Love and Hate in Human Nature.*] *New Republic,* 18 July 1955, 19–20.
"Miro and Modern Art." *Partisan Review* 16 (1949):324–26.
"Muskrat Ramble: Popular and Unpopular Music." *Partisan Review* 15 (1948):614–22. Reprint. Chandler Brossard, ed. *The Scene Before You: A New Approach to American Culture,* 230–38. New York: Rinehart, 1955.
"Robert Motherwell." *Magazine of Art,* March 1948, 86–88.

4. *Psychological Research*
Ruesch, Jurgen, and Weldon Kees. *Non-Verbal Communication: Notes on the Visual Perception of Human Nature.* Berkeley: University of California Press, 1955. Listed as coauthor, Kees actually edited Ruesch's manuscript and supplied approximately half of the three hundred photographs used as illustrations.

SECONDARY SOURCES

Baxter, Charles. "Weldon Kees: The Ghost of American Poetry." In *A Book of Rereadings in Recent American Poetry: 30 Essays.* Edited by Greg Kuzma, Lincoln, Neb. 184–97. Pebble & Best Cellar Press, 1979. Agreeing with Donald Justice that Kees was "one of the bitterest poets in history," Baxter asserts that it "was Kees' special talent to discover how to write passionately, and not just ironically, about this bitterness." Good treatment of Kees's "epistemological bewilderment"—his inability to fit the "pieces" of history and experience together.
————. "Whatever Happened to Weldon Kees?" *Minnesota Review,* Fall 1972, NPR no. 3, 122–26. A highly impressionistic, metaphoric appreciation of Kees, which manages at the same time to be quizzical and praise him in most of the usual ways.
Gioia, Dana. "The Achievement of Weldon Kees." *Sequoia* 29 (1979):25–46. Even if overstated at times, this essay is the most thoughtful article on Kees to date. Combines a general overview with fine and detailed analyses of "1926" and "Aspects of Robinson."

_____. Introduction to *The Ceremony and Other Stories*. Lincoln, Nebr.:
Abattoir Editions, 1983. Fair summary of Kees's short fiction.
Also contains a checklist of Kees's short fiction.

Justice, Donald. Preface to *The Collected Poems of Weldon Kees*. Rev.
ed. Lincoln, Nebr., 1975. Good general introduction. Justice is
especially struck by Kees's profound pessimism and his ability
to wring poetry out of prosaic syntax.

Knoll, Robert E. "Weldon Kees: Solipsist as Poet." *Prairie Schooner*
35 (1961):33–41. Wide-ranging early attempt to assess Kees's
total poetic output. Conclusion is implicit in title: "There is finally
no objective world in these poems. For this mind, the mind is
all that exists."

Libera, Sharon Mayer. "The Disappearance of Weldon Kees."
Ploughshares 15 (1977):147–59. An enthusiastic account of Kees's
poetry by a new admirer.

Mangione, Jerre. *The Dream and the Deal: The Federal Writers' Project,
1935–1943*. Boston: Little, Brown, 1972. As a member of the
Nebraska Writers' Project, Kees is mentioned several times.
Mainly useful for giving an insight into the milieu in which Kees
wrote his short fiction and from which he would have to be graduated to write his poetry—a milieu obsessed with the question
of regionalism. Includes picture of Kees taken in 1940.

Nemerov, Howard. "The Poetry of Weldon Kees." *Poetry and Fiction:
Essays*. New Brunswick, N.J.: Rutgers University Press, 1963.
A review of the Stone Wall Press edition of Kees's poems.

Rexroth, Kenneth. "Weldon Kees." *Assays*. Norfolk, Conn.: New
Directions, 1961. Short appreciation of Kees which describes his
fictional Robinson as "modern man at the end of his rope" and
heaps praise on Kees's unpublished drama, "The Waiting Room."

Sequoia 23 (Spring 1979). An issue devoted to Weldon Kees. Reprints
one of Kees's short stories ("The Ceremony"); also contains
poems in honor of Kees by Art Beck, Dick Davis, Dana Gioia,
Donald Justice, Robert Miklitsch, Hugh Miller, and Lucien Stryk;
reminiscences by Norris Getty and William Jay Smith; short appre-
ciations by Emily Grosholz and Barbara Webber; and a significant
critical study by Dana Gioia, noted above.

Umland, Rudolph. "Lowry Wemberly and Other Recollections of
a Beer Drinker." *Prairie Schooner* 51 (1977):17–50. A recollection
of days spent on the Nebraska Federal Writers' Project. Kees is
mentioned and his Nebraska milieu strikingly evoked.

Index